GRACE AND NECESSITY

REFLECTIONS ON ART AND LOVE

ROWAN WILLIAMS

morehouse

Continuum
The Tower Building
11 York Road
London SE1 7NX

Morehouse
4775 Linglestown Road
Harrisburg
PA 17112

Morehouse is an imprint of Continuum Books

www.continuumbooks.com

First published 2005

British Library Cataloguing-in-Publication Data
A catalogue record for this book is available from the
British Library.

ISBN 0–8192–8118–2

Designed and typeset by Benn Linfield
Printed and bound by MPG Books, Bodmin, Cornwall

CONTENTS

TO THE MASTER
AND FELLOWS
OF TRINITY COLLEGE,
CAMBRIDGE

Introduction

The invitation to deliver the Clark Lectures in 2005 came as both a surprise and a great delight. I was able to explore a theme that had fascinated me for several decades – the relationship between Christian thought and the practice of the arts; more particularly, the interaction between various practising artists and the new and exploratory thinking about aesthetics that was emerging in Roman Catholic thinking in the first quarter of the twentieth century. The term 'neo-scholasticism' is not one calculated to fire the imagination; and the unfashionableness of Thomas Aquinas and his disciples in the wake of the Second Vatican Council, the revulsion both against what was seen as mediaevalism and against the very idea of a comprehensive religious metaphysic, had guaranteed that most of the ideas of this earlier period had fallen into a degree of obscurity. But the work of Jacques Maritain, whose writings form my starting point in what follows, had in its day been novel and even threatening. He was himself, with his extraordinarily gifted and saintly wife, close to the heartlands of European artistic modernism, and his attempt to relate Thomas Aquinas to this world was an enterprise that, I believed, deserved more serious attention than it had generally received.

Maritain's great contribution was twofold. First, he insisted on the integrity of the artwork – its essential independence of any message or propagandist value – and did so on the grounds of a specifically Christian philosophical standpoint. Second, he identified the labour of art as something rooted in the sense of an unfinishedness in 'ordinary' perception, a recognition that the objects of perception were not exhausted by what could be said about them in descriptive, rational and pragmatic terms. It could rightly be said that he is far from original in these claims. To read what he writes about intuition and imagination is to be reminded frequently of Coleridge on the truth-telling and revelatory dimension of imagination – the 'ontology' of art, to use the jargon phrase, art as claiming to have something to say about the fundamental nature of being-in-the-world. But what is distinctive is the anchorage of this in a highly technical metaphysic grounded in Aristotle's rather than Plato's thought, and the careful exploration of the connections and gaps between art and ethical thinking, within a doctrinal framework for which belief in the divine image in humanity and its completion in the Incarnation were central.

Maritain challenged and inspired (and indeed exasperated) many artists. A full survey of his influence would demand a book several times the length of this one. But of those who are most explicit about his impact, I have chosen to concentrate on two: David Jones, poet and painter, and Flannery O'Connor, novelist. Both were very conscious of being Catholic artists; both were intolerant of any suggestion that this obliged them to be edifying or easy. Maritain showed them a way of making sense of what they were doing that was entirely consistent with their beliefs. Indeed, by making the connection between artistic labour and a whole doctrine of being, he allowed them at least to suggest that faith – so far from suppressing creativity – made more and deeper things possible for the artist. The last of the four lectures begins to examine how this might be developed, without too heavy a reliance on the precise vocabulary of Maritain.

Recent discussion of Maritain in English has not been as abundant as his work merits (and I rather hope that the sketchy account here may stimulate more of it); but both David Jones and Flannery O'Connor continue to attract a wealth of scholarly and critical attention. I have not tried to represent the full range of this literature, but have noted, where I thought it helpful, some fuller treatments of themes touched upon in these lectures. I am much indebted to those who have helped my understanding of Jones and O'Connor in various ways over many years, through conversation or correspondence, and by alerting me to various bits of secondary literature; among them especially Donald Allchin, William Blissett, Richard Marsh, D.Z. Phillips and Anne Price-Owen. Warm thanks are also due to all who took part in the discussion that followed each of the lectures; the present text is a somewhat expanded version of what was delivered in Cambridge in February and March of 2005, and I hope that some will recognize in this enlarged text points that they made on these occasions. I am also grateful to Robin Baird-Smith of Continuum for offering to publish the lectures in this form, and for his forbearance and assistance through the process of revision.

But my chief debt, acknowledged in the dedication of this book, is to the Master and Fellows of Trinity College for their kindness in issuing the invitation to deliver these lectures and for their generous encouragement and hospitality throughout. They have helped the performance of this task to be a genuine labour of love.

Rowan Williams

ONE

Modernism
and the Scholastic
Revival

While we are used to the annual ritual controversies around the Turner Prize, and to a modest level of background noise about various acquisitions in the Tate Modern, it would be difficult to claim that serious debate about the nature of visual and plastic art was a particularly visible feature of our intellectual life. As to the verbal arts, poetry, fiction and drama, we (the reasonably educated reader) are fairly familiar with the broad-brush disputes over interpretation generated by postmodernist criticism; we are aware of debates around the significance of theory for the critical appreciation of specific works, around concepts of authorial intention and authority, narrative unity and narrative perspective. We have become used to suspicions about how texts encode patterns of power, often by what they don't say; we can recite the mantras of a certain kind of theory that insists that there is nothing outside the text. But it is unusual to find sustained theoretical reflection on what the process of artistic *composition* entails and what it assumes. Discouraged from large-scale speculation about metaphysics, theories of art have lately shied away from thinking about exactly what kind of *work* creative composition is, and what kind of reality it claims to show or make. Practitioners of visual or verbal art will

3

often write about what they think they are doing; and Heaney or Hill on poetry and Josef Herman's journals on painting offer a wealth of material for the theorist;[1] yet there sometimes seems to be a level of embarrassment among theorists when confronted with such material. And even granted that practitioners do not always know best how to articulate what they are doing, it would be an odd theory that systematically ignored this.

In what follows, I want to examine a particular moment – or series of moments – of encounter between theory and artistic practice, beginning with one sustained attempt to provide a comprehensive theory of artistic labour on the basis of a very ambitious religious metaphysic. It sounds an unpromising beginning in some ways; a religious metaphysic is surely a potently ideological ground for interpretation, offering claims of a totalizing kind that are hostile to the honest practice of art. Yet as a matter of fact this specific metaphysical

1. See, for example: Seamus Heaney, *The Redress of Poetry: Oxford Lectures* (London: Faber, 1995); Geoffrey Hill, *The Lords of Limit. Essays on Literature and Ideas* (London: Andre Deutsch, 1984); Josef Herman, *Related Twilights. Notes from an Artist's Diary*, ed. Tony Curtis (Bridgend: Seren Books, 2002).

essay proved to be a scheme that made sense to a number of practising artists. My aim is to examine briefly what it was that made it so sympathetic to them, and to ask whether there are clues there to a more robust contemporary aesthetic. And one of the serious underlying questions raised by looking at this scheme is whether there is an unavoidably theological element to all artistic labour. That issue is one I shall try to tackle in my final chapter – aware that it suggests an agenda rather more ample than the time available in this context can contain.

Jacques Maritain was one of the central figures of the French Catholic revival at the beginning of the twentieth century. A convert to Catholic Christianity as a young adult, married to an exceptionally gifted woman from a Russian Jewish family, he was close to many of the leading figures in the world of the creative arts over several decades (his wife's memoirs and journals[2] sometimes read

2. Raïssa Maritain, *We Have Been Friends Together* (New York: Longmans, Green and Co., 1942); *Raïssa's Journal*, presented by Jacques Maritain (Albany, New York: Magi Books, 1974). It is worth noting, too, that Gwen John was a near neighbour in Meudon, where the Maritains lived in the 1920s, and for a while was an intimate friend of Raïssa's sister.

---

like a *Who's Who* of the French cultural scene in the twenties). Maritain's relations with Cocteau, for example, constituted an important if inconclusive episode in the lives of both.[3] But Maritain's main intellectual project was the revival of the thought of Thomas Aquinas as the foundation for a contemporary system of political and ethical theory as well as for a religious metaphysic; and from quite early in his career he also set about the construction of a comprehensive aesthetic, a task which came to notable fruition in the 1950s, with the publication of his Mellon Lectures on *Creative Intuition in Art and Poetry*. The revulsion of a great deal of Catholic feeling

3. Raïssa Maritain, *Journal*, pp.182–3. See also Ralph McInerny (below, n.7), pp.100–2, and Francis Steegmuller, *Cocteau. A Biography* (London: David R. Godine, 1992). Maritain more than once quotes Cocteau's comment about authentic art 'guarding the angel' (from *Le Coq et l'Arlequin*); see, for example, p.83 in the collection of Maritain's early writings on aesthetics translated by Victor Scanlon and published as *Art and Scholasticism* (London: Sheed and Ward, 1930) (henceforth AS). The major exchange of correspondence between Maritain and Cocteau is published in the *Cahiers Jean Cocteau* (Paris: Gallimard, 1993), *Correspondence (1923–1963): avec la 'Lettre à Jacques Maritain' et la 'Réponse a Jean Cocteau' (1926)*.

against Thomism in the wake of the Second Vatican Council, and Maritain's own vocal and acerbic criticisms of post-conciliar developments,[4] meant that his monumental system rapidly came to be seen as a museum piece. What is more, the legacy of his political thought proved deeply ambiguous: he was understood as having pro- vided a rationale for Christian Democrat politics, in Europe and in Latin America, a politics devoted to the frustration of open socialism, and a sharp demarcation between the morality of the indi- vidual and the necessarily compromised morality of the state.[5] This is a crassly one-sided reading of Maritain's own political priorities, but it con- tributed to his work being regarded with hostility by many Catholic thinkers of the last quarter of the twentieth century, and eventually to a simple and widespread neglect. The appearance of a full- scale biography in French[6] and a recent and very

4. Most sharply expressed in *The Peasant of the Garonne* (New York: Holt, Rhinehart and Winston, 1968).
5. This critique can be found, for example, in the early work of Gustavo Gutierrez, perhaps the most influen- tial exponent of liberation theology in Latin America in the 1970s.
6. Jean-Luc Barré, *Jacques et Raïssa Maritain. Les mendi- ants du ciel* (Paris: Stock, 1995).

readable survey by Ralph McInerny of Notre Dame[7] have begun to do something to restore his reputation. But many aspects of his work still await proper critical appreciation. Prominent among these, I want to argue, is his aesthetics – not least because of his proximity to some of the most significant currents in what might generally be called literary and artistic modernism in the early twentieth century, understanding 'modern-ism' here as essentially that approach to art that concentrates on the fabric, inner and outer, of the

7. Ralph McInerny, *The Very Rich Hours of Jacques Maritain. A Spiritual Life* (University of Notre Dame Press, 2003). This, like Jude P. Dougherty's useful over-view of Maritain's philosophy *Jacques Maritain: An Intellectual Profile* (Washington: Catholic University of America Press, 2003)), has a very brief account of his aesthetics; otherwise, the fullest study remains, as far as I am aware, John W. Hanke, *Maritain's Ontology of the Work of Art* (The Hague: Martinus Nijhoff, 1973). Ralph McInerny edited a collection of papers on *Art and Prudence: Studies in the Thought of Jacques Maritain* (University of Notre Dame Press, 1989). There is a recent monograph by Francesca Aran Murphy on the aesthetics of the other great French twentieth-century exponent of Thomist philosophy, *Art and Intelligence in the Philosophy of Étienne Gilson* (University of Missouri Press, 2004).

work made rather than any supposed external reference, representational or theoretical.

What Maritain wrote about art reflects a fundamental theme in all his work. His fullest treatise on metaphysics and epistemology has the title *Distinguer pour unir*, 'Distinguishing so as to unite'.[8] He is concerned to clarify the proper sphere of every philosophical discipline and to resist the kind of theological tyranny which assumes that the data of revelation can be brought in as a direct solution to the problems of specific discourses. At one level, this is an acknowledgement of the proper distinction between grace and nature: God makes a world in which created processes have their own integrity, so that they do not need God's constant direct intervention to be themselves. At a deeper level, it assumes a unity between grace and nature: the integrity of a created process will, if pursued honestly and systematically, be open to God's purposes. This formulation conceals one of the bitterest debates of twentieth-century Catholic theology, the controversy that blazed from the 1930s to the 1950s

8. Translated from the fourth French edition as *Distinguish to Unite, or, The Degrees of Knowledge* (London: Geoffrey Bles, 1959).

over the definition of the 'natural' and the 'super-natural'; Maritain, in terms of the theological politics of the period, stood very much along-side those who argued that if grace were really to be God's free gift, the distinction between the natural order of creation and the added dimen-sion of grace had to be absolutely clear. But – without going into the formidable complexities of this question – it would be wrong to think of him as defending a static idea of human activi-ties with goals that are intrinsically unrelated to God. His concern is to suggest how apparently unrelated goals can be understood coherently, so as to avoid that trivializing of human agency that occurs when theological judgements are invoked at the wrong level.[9]

Hence Maritain can say, in his first and most influential essay on aesthetics in general, that art is not *of itself* either grounded in or aimed at moral probity. It is a 'virtue of the practical intellect' – that is, of the mind focused not on knowledge as such but on action. But he also takes for granted

9. A significant early work (first published in French in 1927) that treats this matter in the context of political and social thought is *The Things That Are Not Caesar's* (London: Sheed and Ward, 1930).

here the Aristotelean disjunction, accepted by Aquinas, between the two typical exercises of the practical intellect: it may be oriented to *doing*, to the right use of freedom for the sake of human good, or to *making*, to the production of some specific, determinate outcome, some *product*, in the material world. Virtuous making aims not at the good of humanity but at the good of what is made. Maritain, with conscious mischief, quotes Wilde: 'The fact of a man being a poisoner is nothing against his prose.'[10] As he says in another early essay, art 'is, in a way, an inhuman virtue'.[11] But this statement on its own is misleading: art tends towards beauty, which is what forms in the observer a reaction combining knowledge and delight. Maritain quotes Aquinas's definition of beauty as *id quod visum placet*, 'that which pleases when seen': though he argues that Aquinas's view of beauty is not at all Platonist, since what pleases will vary according to circumstance.[12]

10. AS, p.150, n.20; also in the published version of the Mellon Lectures, *Creative Intuition in Art and Poetry* (henceforth CI), pp.51–2. On art and the practical intellect, see especially AS, p.11 and CI, Chapter 2 *passim*.

11. AS, p.92.

12. AS, pp.23, 28–9; CI, pp.167–76.

What matters is what *this* work requires; a feature
may be in itself jarring or even terrible, but may
still be 'what pleases' in its context. Beauty is
not, therefore, a single transcendent object or
source of radiance. It is a kind of good, but not
a kind of truth – that is, it provides satisfaction,
joy, for the human subject, but does not in itself
tell you anything. Radiance, or what Maritain likes
to call 'splendour', following Aquinas, is the third
level of the life of a finished work. First comes
integrity, the inner 'logic' of a product; then
'proportion' or consonance, its harmony and
adaptation to the observer's receptive mind;
then *splendor* or *claritas*, the active drawing-in of
the observing mind.[13] Beauty, we might paraphrase, is a relation between work and observer
in which the observer's will as well as intellect is
engaged, a relation in which what is present to
the mind is sensed as desirable, as a source of
pleasure. But what Maritain is, I think, cautioning
against is any suggestion that the sensation of
being in the presence of the desirable gives you
any information about how the world actually is
or about what is humanly to be done in it. Given
that the human will is spectacularly fallible and

13. AS, p.24.

self-deceiving, a judgement of beauty cannot as such be morally or metaphysically illuminating.

Yet beauty is not at odds with truth, nor is it an accidental extra in the process of artistic labour. The delight of the subject is in the recognition of what Aquinas calls *splendor formae*, 'splendour of form', a sense of the work achieved as giving itself to the observer in an 'overflow' of presence, the 'radiance' already mentioned. This object is there *for me*, for my delight; but it is so because it is not there *solely* for me, not designed so as to fit my specifications for being pleased. Maritain is not always wholly clear about this, it must be granted; his scheme seems to imply that beauty may exist to some degree independently of a reliable relation with metaphysical depth and truth, and be recognizable even when there is no discernible opening up to this depth. Yet there is also a hint that when we apprehend that something is not there solely for me, that it has an overplus of significance, this very fact has a metaphysical dimension. The emphasis on the gratuity of the artwork, its disinterested character, suggests that the awareness of beauty is always a recognition of what is more than functional in a work, and thus is some kind of relation with an aspect of

reality otherwise unknown. We shall be returning to this theme later. But I suspect here that
Maritain, in his eagerness to distinguish between
knowledge and delight and thus to warn against
an aesthetic reduction of morality (experienced
delight as defining true good) has overstated the
point and obscured something of significance
for his overall argument.

What he is clear about, though, is that the production of beauty cannot be a goal for the artist.
If the artist sets out to please, he or she will
compromise the good of the thing made. If it is
well and honestly made, it will tend towards
beauty – presumably because it will be transpar-
ent to what is always present in the real, that is
the overflow of presence which generates joy. In
the Mellon Lectures, Maritain spells this out a
little more fully, noting that contemporary art is
confused about beauty: either there is a cult of
the beautiful for its own sake, independent of a
clear-headed sense of a work's integrity, or there
is a replacement of beauty by an appeal to a work's
fidelity to the artist's *subjective* integrity – personal
honesty doing duty for formal splendour.[14] Thus

14. CI, pp.183–4.

the great problems of contemporary art are emotionalism and intellectualism: in a highly functionalist culture, the notion of gratuitous beauty becomes deeply problematic, so that a work is judged by its success in stimulating specific feelings or by its capacity to state what is in the artist's mind.[15]

All this helps to explain why Maritain claims in his earlier work that art is more 'intellectual' than prudence – prudence, which is the virtue of practical intellect oriented towards moral virtue, the human good.[16] Art is not about the will – though it unquestionably works on the will. In its actual execution, art does not require good dispositions of the will (poisoners write good prose), nor does it aim to produce good dispositions of the will or indeed *any* particular dispositions of the will. It does not aim at delight or the desire of the good. It seeks the good of *this* bit of work. And the artist as artist is not called on to love God or the world or humanity, but to love what he or she is doing. In a rather extended sense, the activity of the artist *does* have

15. CI, p.195.
16. AS, p.19.

a serious moral character simply because it pushes aside the ego and the desire of the artist as individual. Art is as fundamentally opposed to the will to power as it is to the cult of personality.[17] But in the nature of the case, this happens only when it is not a conscious goal: the will cannot be engaged to will its own banishment. The artist exercises intellect with such detachment that the effect is a sort of image of sanctity, a contemplative absorption in what is truly there. And this needs to be said clearly, not to exalt the status of the artist to that of the saint, but precisely to counter any such idea, any 'messianism' about the artist's role, any slippage towards what the later Maritain calls the magical fallacy of which artists may be victims – that is, the notion that the artist's proper calling is to change the world according to his or her vision.[18]

Yet the artist's work is inescapably a claim about reality. It is not, that is to say, a new world depending on the play of an individual psyche any more than it is the expression of a specific project of the artist's will. 'Poetry is ontology',

17. CI, pp.231–2.
18. CI, pp.144–5, 184ff.

Maritain asserts in his essay on 'The Frontiers of Poetry', it has to do with our knowledge of being itself.[19] Any poetic utterance, any visible or tangible object made by art, is already a metaphysical statement. The argument seems to be roughly this: art is not a matter of deciding to create this or that pattern, because that would reduce it to an act of will; but if it is more to do with intelligence than will, it is bound to be exercised in relation to what is actual, since intelligence, in Maritain's Thomist philosophical scheme, is necessarily oriented towards being.[20] The practical intellect is a way of 'coping' with what is actually there – that's what makes it practical. Art therefore is bound to show what is in some sense real; it shows something other than its own labour of creation. 'The normal climate of art is intelligence and knowledge', as Maritain wrote in the Mellon Lectures;[21] and earlier he had spoken of the 'antinomy' of all art as a negotiating of the tension between an 'essential reality' and the actual facts of the world: art seeks to reshape the data of the world so as to make their fundamental

19. AS, p.91.
20. See, for example, Chapter 3 of *The Degrees of Knowledge*, especially pp.77ff.
21. CI, p.64.

structure and relation visible.[22] Thus the artist *does* set out to change the world, but – if we can manage the paradox – to change it into itself.

This is why art can never be simply imitative. When there is a trend towards the imitative, there will inevitably be a reaction in the direction of conceptualism: cubism emerges from the reaction against what Maritain calls the 'theatrical' mistakes of nineteenth-century realism and Impressionism.[23] Properly, art 'spreads over [things] a secret which it first discovered in them, in their invisible substance or in their endless exchanges and correspondences'.[24] But again, when the artist becomes so absorbed in those initially invisible structures as to lose touch with the actuality of objects, he or she is inevitably frustrated: God alone sees and knows structures in themselves by his eternal 'ideas' of the world; but for finite mind and imagination, there is always the link with actual perception of finite objects. The artist struggling for perfect abstract expression is trying to imitate God's self-sufficiency; the surrealist struggling to lay out the movement of

22. AS, p.90.
23. AS, pp.54–5.
24. AS, p.96.

thought or language as such, independent of the act of intelligible communication, is likewise engaged in a 'promethean' enterprise.[25] I suspect that Maritain would not have wanted to be understood as condemning abstract art unreservedly; after all, the 'abstract' still works with the concrete relations of colour and physical shape, and to read, say, Malevich on the nature of visual art is to find something not by any means alien to some of Maritain's concerns.[26] But the warning is more directed to the self-understanding of the

25. CI, pp.73–82.
26. Kasimir Malevich's 'suprematism' was a significant presence in the Russian artistic world at the beginning of the twentieth century, seeking to expose the relations of items and levels of the world to each other by the deployment of coloured geometrical forms. He had moved on from an early residual realism to a cubist phase and finally to a commitment to abstract composition intended to be divorced from 'nature'. But his writing reflects a deep and confused spiritual apprehension, a search for some attunement to underlying harmonics. *The Non-objective World* is the title of an English translation of some of his theoretical work (published in Chicago in 1960). Camilla Gray, *The Russian Experiment in Art, 1863–1922* (London: Thames and Hudson, 1971 (2nd edn)), remains a good guide to Malevich and his contemporaries.

abstract artist: whatever this created object is, it is not something *directly* rooted in or related to the structures of intelligible reality in a way that bypasses the given material world. The artist only reflects the thoughts of God as they are embodied in this actual environment.[27]

In 'Frontiers of Poetry' Maritain traces this particular temptation, this artistic 'sin of the angels', as he puts it, to the cultural moment in which the artist becomes fully self-conscious – the Renaissance.[28] The more the artist is aware of laying bare the invisible, the more there may grow a passion to express in the work all that the artist's mind conceives. This may be, as we have seen, a matter of the perception of abstract structure; but it may equally be, in the absence of a clear sense of *any* externally given reality, intellectual or material, an urgency to express the individual self without reserve. Maritain speaks, in a striking phrase, of Rimbaud's 'eucharistic passion': the inevitable failure to allay this passion for total self-embodiment, for the 'transubstantiation' of the self into words, leads to blasphemy

27. CI, Chapter 3 *passim*.
28. AS, p.100.

and despair.[29] Mallarmean 'pure poetry' leads to
an aesthetic crisis. It is an artistic moment of
truth, in that the artist has to decide whether the
end of the process is unavoidable tragic frustration – so that this itself becomes the matter of
poetry – or a contemplative orientation towards
what is never going to be contained, the world
in the eyes of God. Again, this is a question to
which we shall be returning. The mature Maritain,
in the Mellon Lectures, speaks of finite beauty or
finishedness in the work being always incomplete at some level, 'limping', like the biblical
Jacob, from the encounter with what cannot be
named; achieved art always has '*that kind* of
imperfection through which infinity wounds the
finite'.[30]

Gradually the nature of art's metaphysical claim
comes more fully into focus. Art challenges the
finality of appearance here and now, the actual
'conditions of existence', not in order to destroy
but to ground, amplify, fulfil. It aims at 'transcend-
ental realism'. Without this basis, it becomes either
the transcription of a particular psychological

29. AS, p.101.
30. CI, pp.166–7.

agenda or a conceptual system set up in rivalry to the specific actuality that the artist faces. Both errors simplify the complex relations of labour and transformation that issue in finished or 'beautiful' work (granted the flexibility of what 'beauty' means here). Because of its character as an act of intellect rather than will, art aims always at the formally finished work (granted what has just been said about the necessary unfinishedness at another level of any form created by the artist), not at the stimulating of particular felt response: it speaks to intelligence, inviting intelligence to recognize its truth. It demands – in an extended but still exact sense – contemplation, the intellect being shaped by the impress of truth in such a way that the impress of truth on the artistic mind or imagination is continued through the work (but *only* through the work, not through an idea that can be abstracted from the work or through the artist's gloss on their own production). And in all these ways, the work not only challenges appearances; it challenges pre-existing assumptions about knowledge itself. It makes claims about being but also about how being is adequately known. In the light of this, we need to look at what Maritain has to say about the actual intellectual process that is artistic composition.

2

The earlier Maritain is fairly sketchy about these specifics, though there are hints; the developed doctrine is to be found in the Mellon Lectures.[31] Here he begins with the broad assertion that the poetic (by implication the artistic in general) represents the communion between the inner life of the objects of the world and the human self; it is a level of intellection at which the conventional bounds between world and subject are breached (so that it can be described as a purified form of magic). Because it transgresses the ordinary bounds of conscious intellectual activity, its roots must be located in the *preconscious* life of the intellect – a central concept for the lectures.[32]

What this means is spelled out in the third and fourth lectures particularly. Every human subject is in touch with the 'illuminating intellect', the reflection of God's formative mental activity within our own: below the surface of human mental agency, Maritain is saying, lies a kind of participatory awareness, a contact not yet expressed in

31. CI, Chapters 3, 4 and 8 in particular.
32. CI, pp.71ff.

word or concept, that resonates with the patterns of God's action in the created world. 'Spiritual forms', concepts, intelligible patterns in our apprehending of the world, are the result of the intellectual action of God drawing and moulding our mental action so as to generate coherent images that encode or even 'embody' the rhythms of God's working. This is not simply a registering of some world of impressions outside the subject: we have to take the language of 'impression' absolutely seriously and think about the self as showing the reality it encounters through the perceptible effect upon it of the agency of an other. To be aware of the self is to be aware of something that bears the marks of otherness, not of a pristine independent subjectivity. My intellection is – in the Germanic phrase – 'always already' addressed, impressed, illuminated; but therefore also acting upon, processing and transforming raw data. There is never a confrontation between those two mythological entities of modern epistemology – the innocent receptacle of the disinterested mind and the uninterpreted data of external reality. The mind is itself already an agency with a 'shape', a tendency to respond thus and not otherwise; it makes patterns of what it confronts according to the patterning it

24

has received in its primordial contact with God's agency. The artist's knowledge is a kind of self-knowledge.[33] And, as Maritain elaborates in the first of the Mellon Lectures, ultimately an art concentrating on things (as in the pre-modern world or the Orient) can't help but reveal the creative self, and an art concentrated on the self (as in Western modernity) can't help but reveal the depth of things.[34] There is a 'cunning of reason' in the creative process, we might say; and Maritain is more optimistic here than in his earlier work about how even a deeply individualistic and anti-transcendental art cannot completely frustrate some kind of openness to unseen structures.

But this in turn means that the way in which the developed conscious mind maps the world is only an aspect of a deeper and more mysterious relationship between mind and world. Our habitual mental working rests on the relations between a conceptualized bit of the material environment and the conscious conceptual structures that tell you as an intellectual subject how to approach, understand and find your way around it. But these are not the only relationships in which the

33. CI, pp.113–14.
34. CI, p.33.

elements in that environment are involved. In one of the most significant phrases of this discussion, Maritain speaks of how 'things are not only what they are', how they 'give more than they have'.[35] Hence, of course, the uselessness of ordinary realism: to represent what is there in what he has called the 'theatrical' mode, to reproduce a world in a way that takes for granted where its boundary lines are drawn by our ordinary conceptual mapping, is to fail radically in the artistic task, which is to open up knowledge otherwise unavailable. This is the context in which Maritain denies so forcefully that a product of art is the embodiment of an artist's idea.[36]

As we shall see in other connections, this entails the possibility of what can be quite dramatic strategies in 'challenging appearances'; and it gives further substance to Maritain's careful qualifications about the sorts of beauty appropriate to different works. To make present the underlying structures and relations apprehended may involve a degree of imaginative violence to surface harmonies. The danger for art is not in the production of the shocking or the jarring, but in

35. CI, p.127.
36. CI, pp.136–7.

the pursuit of what is shocking as an exercise of the artistic will; a complex discernment is required here. The deliberate cultivation of what jars is as much a folly, artistically, as the deliberate striving for beauty. The issue is always and only about the integrity of the work. The artist first listens and looks for the pulse or rhythm that is not evident; but she cannot do any sort of job if she refuses to work with such pulses.[37]

Maritain's own word is 'pulsions', a notion he discusses in the last two of the lectures, and whose definition clearly causes him some trouble.[38] He wants to argue that what lies at the root of specifically poetic labour is what he calls a 'musical stir', an intuition of something like rhythm – a connection that owes something to the insights of his wife, Raïssa, who wrote a good deal of poetry.[39] And this 'intuitive pulsion' is what is most essential to poetry. Historically speaking, poetry has regularly worked with the music of actual sounds, the patterning of words in rhyme or metre, but modern poetry does not assume that this is necessary. Instead, modern poetry pushes

37. CI, Chapter 8 *passim*.
38. CI, pp. 302ff.
39. See, for example, *Raïssa's Journal*, p.349.

us back towards the deeper 'pulsions' – which seem, from the examples Maritain gives (from Baudelaire and, a little strangely, given his attention to strictly verbal music, Hopkins), to be something like units of imaginative sense, clusters of feeling or even 'knots' of imagery and cross-reference, which can never be captured simply in the music of sounds.[40] Perhaps the haiku would be a paradigm of what is at the centre of composition thus understood.

What he seems to be saying is that the poetic process is first a kind of apprehending of the environment that blurs conventional boundaries of perception – not to dissolve the actuality that is there but to bring out relations and dimensions that ordinary rational naming and analysing fail to represent. Perhaps more than this, it is a sense of objects as it were carrying with them a charge of feeling that links them to other objects. Thus Proust's generative moment might be a paradigm of one aspect of this 'musical' apprehension. It is the level of awareness at which metaphor is inescapable, the level at which my sense of an object and its intrinsic life are indistinguishable. That is

40. CI, pp.313–24.

why poetry can be said to have roots in magical and mythological consciousness. The contemporary poet is, in a more self-aware fashion, recreating that consciousness, in deliberate transgression of ordinary contemporary canons of rational description.

It is interesting that Maritain speaks consistently of 'music' in this context, but refuses to identify poetic music with patterns of sounds. He is, I think, proposing an analogy between music as the development of intrinsic relations and proportions in the world of sound, and poetry as the laying bare of relations and proportions in the ensemble of what is perceived over and above (or below) the register in which we talk of self-contained entities. It is all to do with things 'being more than they are'. Metaphor implies that diverse, sometimes very diverse, items in the perceptual field can be related as if they were on the same 'frequency': something about the life of this object in action shares the same style of action as is seen in something different. Or, in an older and more technical idiom, metaphor suggests *participation* between different agencies. Once again, there is a metaphysical point being indirectly made (scholastic thought insists that knowing is always a form of participation in the active intelligible life of an object, reproducing itself in the life of the subject; this is simply to take the pattern to a level unfamiliar to classical scholastic thought).[41] And the point can be translated into talking about the visual arts in some very interesting ways, as we shall see in the next of these lectures.

This is why, incidentally, Maritain can insist[42] that the surface meaning of a poem (or, presumably, any product of art) may be accessible and clear or the opposite, without this affecting its clarity *as a work*. The obscurity or indeterminacy of a poem at the intellectual level can indeed be a strength, since it becomes free to signify more to the reader. Maritain refers to Eliot's *Ash Wednesday* as an instance of poetic clarity – in a way that Eliot himself would have happily endorsed. When asked by an undergraduate what he meant by 'Lady, three white leopards sat under a juniper tree', he famously replied, 'I mean, "Lady, three white leopards sat under a juniper

---

41. CI, pp.117f.; and cf. Chapter 5 of *The Degrees of Knowledge*.
42. AS, p.59; CI, pp.257–68.

tree"'.[43] The signification of the words is neither conceptual nor representational; it is the positing of a world in which these words 'catch' and establish certain relations or resonances.

43. Stephen Spender, 'Remembering Eliot', in Allen Tate (ed.) *T. S. Eliot: The Man and his Work* (London: Penguin, 1971) (pp.42–68), p. 46.

3

Just in case this appears too much of an essay in scholastic epistemology gone slightly off the rails, it may be worth noting in comparison some of what recent analytic writers and practitioners have had to say about the poetic process. In a paper on 'Wordless words: poetry and the symmetry of being', Michael Maltby, a clinical psychologist, has outlined a theoretical perspective on poetic awareness that strikingly echoes some of Maritain's scheme.[44] He is dissatisfied with the kind of psychoanalytic tradition of interpretation that sees artistic activity as essentially a matter of the 'economics' of the psyche – the utilizing of repressed material. From Freud onwards, there has been something of an analytic orthodoxy, variously expressed, on this. The formation of the self in and through language requires the imposition of order, so that certain forms of consciousness – what Kristeva calls the 'semiotic' as opposed to the 'symbolic' – are denied. Art (especially in verbal form) restores the semiotic by disrupting the order of habitual consciousness.

44. In Hamish Canham and Carole Satyamurti (eds), *Acquainted With The Night. Psychoanalysis and the Poetic Imagination* (London and New York: Karnac, 2003).

'Semiotic' here refers to a process of communication by signs that is not yet reduced to regularity and stability; what 'counts' in this stage is something more fluid. So the return of the repressed in art recovers 'metaphor, metonymy and musicality' as ways of accessing that fluid, timeless mode of knowing in which we do not have to generalize or universalize but only to enter into the resonance of the moment.[45]

But this takes us only so far. It misses out on the artist's labour to shape, from the buried material of 'semiotic' awareness, an intelligible product; and it makes art ultimately functional, a release of tension, rather than an action undertaken for its own sake – or, better, as a deliberate attempt to display the reality that the intelligence as a whole encounters. Maltby turns to the very sophisticated scheme proposed by another analytic theorist, Ignacio Matte-Blanco, for an alternative.[46] In this, preconscious/subconscious thought is characterized as 'symmetric':

45. Maltby, p.54.
46. See Ignacio Matte-Blanco, *Thinking, Feeling and Being* (London: Routledge, 1988); also Rodney Bomford, *The Symmetry of God* (London: Free Association Books, 1999), Chapter 3 on Matte-Blanco.

objects present themselves in certain 'sets' that are not the same as those we use in ordinary practical discrimination (where we need to know what the differences are between objects so that we can act appropriately and successfully in relation to them). The language of cause and effect does not routinely apply in this context, and conventional assumptions about boundaries and exclusions in what we say about the world are absent. A perceiving mind that operated solely in a symmetric way would be pathological, dysfunctional. But this is often the result of consciousness's efforts to do without the symmetric, to deny or refuse the knowledge that is available at this level. In other words, thinking that is completely asymmetric, using a logic of exclusions and regular causalities, is as 'abnormal' as thinking that is completely symmetrical. Neither can live in the other's absence.

Poetry is a fusion of symmetric and asymmetric. It depends on the possibility of establishing perceptions of identity in the world that do not depend on stable verbal definition. 'Identities can be established in terms of sound, image, or pattern of movement. Identities established at that level can, in turn, be differentiated in terms below a level of verbal statement.'[47] Maltby's example is Auden's 'Night Mail' as an enactment of perception working below the level of *statement*. I am not sure if this is the best or most resourceful example, as it does not go very much beyond a reproduction of a particular ordered set of impressions (imitating the rhythm of the train). But the point is clear enough; and a richer example might be, perhaps, Rilke's 'Duino Elegies', with their symphonic movements of emotional tone, working at a far more fundamental level than any verbal argument; or, as suggested earlier, and on a very different scale from Rilke's massive edifices, the haiku. And this prompts some thoughts on what a translator of poetry might be about and whether it is absolutely true that poetry perishes in translation: if a translator catches the music not of the words, which is impossible to reproduce, but of the 'symmetric' complexes of image and feeling, what emerges is still poetry. Christopher Logue's extraordinary renditions of Homer are a case in point here.[48]

It should be clear that this is not a digression from our main enterprise of elucidating Maritain.

47. Maltby, p.63.
48. See *Logue's Homer: Cold Calls* (London: Faber, 2005).

He predictably avoids the language of the sub-conscious; but his 'preconscious' in fact works in a closely similar way. The analogy of music is powerfully present in both the neo-scholastic and the analytic discussions, but in both it refers to something other than the mere sound of the words. Both end up with a view of poetry which sees it as a work of intelligence, a practice of knowing, that precariously straddles the bound-aries of two sorts of mental activity. Both agree in seeing it as something more than an inten-sified representation on the one hand and a Dionysiac self-expression on the other. If it is indeed the return of the repressed, this should not be taken as simply an act of release or of sub-limation that has no implications for questions of truth.

So with this in mind, we can begin to draw together some of the essentials of Maritain's aes-thetic. Much of the argument has been about poetry, but its applicability to visual art is not difficult to explain. The leading themes are these:

(i)   Art is an action of the intelligence and thus makes claims about how things are.

(ii) As such, it invites contemplation; that is, it sets out to create something that can be absorbed by intelligence, rather than a tool for use in a project larger than itself.

(iii) Thus the canons for understanding art must relate to the integrity of what is being produced, not to goals extrinsic to this process of labour.

(iv) When art engages the will by its own integrity and inner coherence, we speak of its beauty; but beauty cannot be sought as something in itself, independent of what *this* work demands.

(v) By engaging us in an unforeseen pattern of coherence or integrity, art uncovers relations and resonances in the field of perception that 'ordinary' seeing and experiencing obscure or even deny.

(vi) Thus art in one sense 'dispossesses' us of our habitual perception and restores to reality a dimension that necessarily escapes our conceptuality and our control. It makes the world strange.

(vii) So, finally, it opens up the dimension in which 'things are more than they are', 'give more than they have'. Maritain is circumspect in spelling out the implication of this, but it is pretty clear that what this means is that art necessarily relates in some way to 'the sacred', to energies and activities that are wholly outside the scope of representation and instrumental reason.

From all these, we can also draw a clear picture of what Maritain believes *fails* as art. Realism is a regular target for his polemic; so is edification. Art does not seek to reproduce items of ordinary consciousness; it is bound to the actuality of its own material medium and seeks to make something that is in accord with that medium, so that it cannot properly try to *overcome* its own matter. *Trompe-l'oeil* is not the purpose of art. In this, incidentally, Maritain's efforts to show that Aristotle's idea of art as mimesis are wholly compatible with his own scheme are none too successful.[49] Equally, art as propaganda, its workings determined by the purpose of persuading those who see and hear of a message that can be separated from the actual work, is a nonsense. It would mean that the artist was not thinking first of the good of what is being made, but treating this as an extra to the task of rhetoric. This emphatically

49. AS, p.58.

does not mean that art makes no claims relating to truth or goodness. Nor does it mean that the artist as such is devoid of metaphysical conviction or of the passion to share it. The artist produces what his habits of perception permit, and those habits are moral and metaphysical as well as narrowly perceptual.

Maritain is far from claiming that there are no moral questions to be asked of artistic production, but his argument needs some teasing out. A bad man may produce fine work; but there is a precariousness in this. The ineptitude of a person's moral perception is a factor that can easily spill over into other ineptitudes. A bad man whose badness takes the shape of self-centred exploitation of his material to advance his personality is a bad artist .[50] And that habit of self-centredness is unlikely to be simply a matter of artistic practice, but connected with or rooted in other moral failures. The artist as artist has a morality, and it is not wholly divorced from the rest of what constitutes morality. What Maritain is saying is, I think, that in our total response to the artistic

50. E.g., AS, p.38, CI, pp.144–5, on the essential disinterestedness of the artist.

product, the engagement of our will in recognizing beauty means that we are inevitably caught up at some point in a judgement of whether the world that the work sets before us is desirable. This does not determine our judgement of how the work works, so to speak, its integrity and resonance. But the question of whether a world laid before us by an artist is desirable *for the kind of creatures we know ourselves to be* is a larger and a necessary one. If we have no conception of what kind of creatures we are, then we shall have little or nothing to help us with that judgement, and art becomes a carnival of the uneducated passions. Not only is there nothing to be said about the badness of artists producing good work, there is nothing ultimately to be said about the moral disposition of the artists towards the work, and we shall have no means of speaking about the good at all. The mistake Maritain is concerned to counter is not a link between art and the good, but a reduction of the former to the latter, so that good art is simply the production of material designed to make us desire the good. Bad men make good things; but good men also make bad things, works that are intrinsically dishonest and empty, because they do not keep their eyes on the good of the work – even when they have a sound conception of what is good for the sort of beings we are. *Distinguer pour unir* once again; we only grasp the way in which art and morality connect when we know exactly why and how they are not the same. And both are damaged when we fail to do this.

Maritain's reflections on art are, I have suggested, one of the most abidingly interesting and fresh aspects of his complex system. But the plausibility of any aesthetic has a lot to do with whether practitioners can recognize what is being talked about as the sort of thing they actually do. One of the most striking features of the reception of Maritain's thinking is the enthusiasm displayed by working artists for his ideas. It would be intriguing to trace that reception among artists who had little or no theological commitment; but his work was clearly most liberating for those who had to struggle against assumptions about religious art that were essentially hostile to the very idea of art. In the next two lectures, I shall be looking at two of these in particular, David Jones and Flannery O'Connor – a poet and draughtsman, and a writer of fiction. For both, Maritain was of decisive significance. But they also suggest why this account of the nature of art itself has some apologetic interest; and the final lecture will address aspects of this. For if things 'give more than they have' in the artist's world, what exactly can be said about that redundancy and excess of gift that does not sooner or later have to connect with a picture of divine *poiesis*?

Two

David Jones:
Material Words

Maritain's *Art et scholastique* was translated into English in 1923, under the title *The Philosophy of Art*, by Joseph O'Connor – best remembered as the prototype for Chesterton's Father Brown. O'Connor, a parish priest in Bradford, had a notable rapport with artists and writers; and at this time he was closely involved with Eric Gill, whose confessor he was over many years (no sinecure, as readers of Gill's biography will be aware).[1] The translation was done in substantial part at Ditchling in Sussex, where Gill had lived since 1907; it was published by the St Dominic's Press, which Gill had established in association with Hilary Pepler some seven years earlier. The essay made an immediate and profound impact on Gill and the little community of artists and craftsmen around him, and decisively shaped a great deal of Gill's later writing

1. Fiona McCarthy, *Eric Gill* (London: Faber, 1989). The revelations in this book about Gill's omnivorous sexuality paint a significantly different picture from that in the earlier biography by Robert Speaight (*The Life of Eric Gill* (London: Methuen, 1966)); but this latter (by a personal friend of Gill's) is still a more thorough guide to some of Gill's ideas.

on art.[2] Up to that point, he had had exposure to some elements of scholastic philosophy through his contacts with the English Dominicans, especially Fr Vincent McNabb,[3] but perhaps the most important intellectual influence had been Ananda Coomaraswamy, the most sophisticated exponent to Western audiences in his day of a pre-modern, oriental and hieratic philosophy of art.[4] Gill always acknowledged this debt; but it was the vocabulary of Maritain that most marked him. After 1923, he could claim that his ideas about art were fully in tune with the foremost contemporary interpreter of Aquinas, and so with the essence of Catholic philosophy.

2. McCarthy describes Maritain's book as 'very much the handbook of that period at Ditchling' (p.161). Jonathan Miles, *Eric Gill and David Jones at Capel-y-ffin* (Bridgend: Seren Books, 1992), Chapter 4, has a good overview of Maritain's impact on Gill at this time. See also Rowan Williams, 'Eric Gill', *Sobornost* 1977, 261–9 for a summary of Gill's aesthetics.

3. On Vincent McNabb, see Ferdinand Valentine, *Father Vincent McNabb, OP: the Portrait of a Great Dominican* (London: Burns and Oates, 1955).

4. See the collection of Coomaraswamy's papers on aesthetics edited by Roger Lipsey, *Coomaraswamy. Vol.1. Selected Papers: Traditional Art and Symbolism* (Princeton University Press, 1977).

Gill's first exercise in rendering Maritain into his own terms was his 1925 essay, *Id Quod Visum Placet* – the title taking up Aquinas's definition of beauty, which, as we have seen, Maritain had made his own.[5] He takes as foundational the principle that art aims at the good of the thing made – so that an artistic product is an object made *in* the chosen medium, not an imitation or reproduction of something else; consequently it is a mistake to aim at beauty as if it were anything other than the effect of the work's integrity. In the many essays that followed, especially in the years up to 1933, and in his voluminous correspondence, Gill elaborated his assimilation of Maritain's themes. 'Art is skill', he wrote, a habit nurtured by practical apprenticeship which develops a natural capacity;[6] we do not need any doctrine of mysterious giftings, spiritual genius, in an artist. The truest art is anonymous; emotions are never the ground of artistic work, only some of the consequences; 'high art' or 'fine art' is essentially a distraction, and the bulk of post-Renaissance art is a disaster. It has encouraged

5. *Id Quod Visum Placet* (Waltham St Lawrence: Golden Cockerel Press, 1926).
6. Eric Gill, *Beauty Looks After Herself* (London: Sheed and Ward, 1933), p.11.

us to think of painting not as a sharing in the creative labour of God for the world's eventual fulfilment but as the record of a particular individual sensibility *looking* at the world from outside.[7] True art is in some sense a part of nature, nature in its human embodiment pursuing its natural intellectual and formative character.[8] Art is 'metaphysically superior' to prudence in its aspiration to collaboration with God. But prudence is more important for the human being as such, more in tune with what human beings concretely are and need. The two exist in a perpetual 'lover's quarrel' (art being male and prudence female): prudence is suspicious of art's concern with things in themselves, art is equally suspicious of prudence's utilitarianism.[9] We are lost if we try to separate the two: the truth is that prudence aims at the true good of human beings, but that true good includes, crucially,

7. Ibid., p.89; cf. pp.91–2 on the failure of post-Renaissance art to see paintings as things rather than 'viewpoints'.
8. See, e.g., Walter Shewring (ed.), *Letters of Eric Gill* (London: Jonathan Cape, 1947), pp.86ff.; cf. *Beauty Looks After Herself*, p.165 (art does not reproduce nature but works as she works).
9. *Beauty Looks After Herself*, pp.16–19.

happiness. And 'happiness is the state of being *pleased* with things, of being pleased with *things*').[10] Art must aim at products that please the whole person. And the good of the whole person is something specified by that doctrine to which prudence tries to conform us. In the terms used in the previous chapter, art is good when it relates to the sort of creatures we know ourselves to be.

For Gill, while the artist as concretely engaged in the work is not as such a propagandist (because concerned about the good of the work and nothing else), the work itself must be in some sense propaganda: 'Art which is not propaganda is simply aesthetics.'[11] It must be done in the service of a community with a clear shared ideology (which is why the right relation of art and prudence is impossible in contemporary society where the artist is reduced to being an entertainer); it must be a matter of performing tasks prescribed for the good of the community, so that it offers what is pleasing to the rightly oriented perception and emotion of persons in the community. Hence the impossibility – as in the

10. Ibid., pp.26–7.
11. *Letters*, p.309.

Middle Ages – of distinguishing clearly between
the artist and the craftsman, and the evils of
post-Renaissance art with its mystique of the
artist-genius, the solitary visionary.[12] And in a
situation of massive and endemic social injustice
(Gill never lost his early passion about the evils
of capitalist modernity), the priority must be to
liberate the great mass of people to exercise their
proper creativity in making things rather than to
encourage fantasies about genius: 'It will be time
enough to worry about the place of the Beeth-
ovens, Shakespeares and Dostoevskys when Tom,
Dick and Harry and you and me have established the Kingdom of God and His justice, if
ever.'[13] Gill's artistic theory is inseparable from his
vision of a society in which every working man
(the male pronoun is deliberate) participates in
the free exercise of intelligent making, instructed
by the canons of virtuous doing so that he
knows the purpose of what he makes.

And this is the point at which Gill's reading of
Maritain becomes a fascinating distortion.
Maritain is clear that art and prudence are not

12. See the essay on 'Paintings and criticism', *Beauty Looks
    After Herself*, pp.84–94, and cf. Speaight, p.193.
13. Ibid., p.381.

50

ultimately separable, and that the artist as human being is bound to have ideological commitments and moral concerns. But what cannot be extracted from his work is anything like Gill's doctrine of the artist as producing according to the specified needs of a community. It would be wrong to say that Gill simply subordinates art to external control: the execution of any work remains strictly ordered by the nature of the thing made. But there is more than a hint that 'the nature of the thing made' is, in the ideal cultural setting, known in advance in the light of a shared philosophy. The fact that this assumption would not be out of place in the high days of Soviet Russia would probably not have upset Gill very much; Soviet Russia had the wrong philosophy, objectively (though not as wrong as some people thought), but the right attitude to the place of cultural making in society.[14] Maritain, though, is resistant to the idea that art is a making of objects known beforehand in some way: the artist obeys the 'laws' of what is being made, certainly, but this should not be confused with any notion of an authority telling the artist what to make. And

14. See Speaight, *op. cit.*, pp.238ff. on Gill's attitudes to Communism, and 273ff. on the Spanish Civil War.

51

the ultimate, global judgement of any work is indeed inseparable from its congruence with what we objectively are as humans; but that congruence has to be discovered by patient attention to the particularity of what is made, even and especially when it does not instantly appear to fit in with a functional notion of what will edify or inspire. In the next chapter we shall see how important this was for a writer of fictions that were anything but conventionally edifying. The maker's obedience is to the integrity of the thing made, to the unfolding logic in the process of making, as the work discloses itself – not to a close specification of what is *needed*. Gill's model suggests that there is no real gratuity in the artist's making; he comes curiously close to a quite drastic functionalism in his insistence that ideally the community determines what the artist's business shall be.

Gill was described on his tombstone, according to his own wishes, simply as 'Stone Carver'; as we have seen, he could make little of the distinction between artist and craftsman, and was relentlessly hostile to anything in which he detected what he liked to call 'art nonsense' (the title of one of his collections of essays). But this savage reaction against both art as entertainment and art as a mysterious end in itself leaves entirely out of consideration what is perhaps Maritain's most significant contribution to the whole debate: his analysis of art as exposing the 'excess' of the material environment ('things are more than they are'). Certainly Gill speaks of the artist as – so to speak – contributing to nature, continuing the work of God in the world, recreating objects in another medium, not copying them. He can define art – in terms taken up enthusiastically by David Jones – as the one 'intransitive' activity of human beings, the one thing not designed to solve predefined problems.[15] But he seems not to recognize the tension between this and the stringent communal and ideological context he thinks necessary for art to be fully itself.

15. The expression is quoted by Jones in his essay, 'Art in relation to war', reprinted in Harman Grisewood (ed.), *The Dying Gaul and Other Writings* (London: Faber, 1978), p.161. It sits uncomfortably with much of Gill's work; but Gill seems to be saying that human beings are *capable* of this intransitive activity, even if the exercise of it in a strictly intransitive way ('art for art's sake') is not proper to the mature human moral agent.

Aspects of his own practice cast light on this unresolved area. He was, of course, a supremely professional producer of material things, working to commission. What made sense to him in Maritain was the conviction that his job was not to express himself or to make pleasurable objects in a vacuum. Yet it is hard not to feel that much of his work falls between several stools. His commissions were frequently for essentially *decorative* objects – the famous Broadcasting House statue of Prospero and Ariel, the Leeds University frieze, the illustrations for limited editions of books published by small presses. The sculpture, as has often been remarked, is overwhelmingly an exercise in the handling of surface rather than volume. His brilliance at creating typefaces is an outstanding instance of the production of things that combine utility with beauty; but it is not an obvious example of art sharing in the self-propagation of nature. 'He side-stepped modernism' is the judgement of a perceptive recent critic.[16] Despite his endorsement of Maritain's principle, so close to the heart of the modernist aesthetic, that the made object is its own 'world' of reference, what he means by this is a deeply

16. Jonathan Miles, *op. cit.*, p.76.

un-modernist belief about the ideal primacy of hieratic convention, almost of ritual function, within a society of clear and uniform conviction. In the context of a very different kind of society, the result is immensely skilled work, often genuinely bold, witty, or monumental and poignant; but the tone-deafness about gratuity and about the formally exploratory nature of artistic production ironically leaves him stuck between the utilitarian and the decorative, a theologian inexorably condemned to appear as an entertainer. Remembering Maritain's dictum about the incompleteness of authentic art, its woundedness by the infinite, we might wonder where the wounds are in Gill.

2

Some of the most sympathetic but candid discussion of the depth of Gill's anti-modernism and the problems and dangers of his craftsmanlike elegance in dealing with a surface, whether for carving or for engraving, can be found in a couple of brief essays by David Jones written very soon after Gill's death.[17] Characteristically, Jones sees Gill, for all his passionate reformism, as basically untroubled by the seriousness of the cultural crisis of modernity. As Gill's first biographer noted,[18] he was not a man to whom you could ascribe much in the way of 'negative capability', and there is a sense in which Gill's reaction to modernity is therefore a flat denial, not a negotiation. Jones, in contrast,

17. 'Eric Gill as sculptor' and 'Eric Gill, an appreciation', reprinted in David Jones, *Epoch and Artist. Selected Writings*, ed. Harman Grisewood (London: Faber, 1959), pp.288–302. It is worth noting one of Jones's phrases in the first of these pieces: Gill 'sometimes spoiled works by "completing" them in some technical sense' (p.293). This throws further light on the question of whether Gill shows anything of what I have called the woundedness of art.
18. Speaight, p.228.

accepts the diagnosis of a cultural dead end, but wrestles painfully with how to pursue an honest artistic path in this actual environment. Yes, we are all now heirs of the 'decadence' of the 1890s, in that we are all involved in 'an exasperated search for beauty on the part of individual men conscious or unconscious of the declining West'.[19] We have no culture that educates us *as* artists; and it is no use pretending that we have or can simply retreat into another cultural frame. The painfulness of being aware of this is a theme that recurs in Jones's work, not least in the famous little fragment, '*A,a,a, Domine Deus*', written and revised over a period of nearly 30 years: 'I have been on my guard not to condemn the unfamiliar./For it is easy to miss Him at the turn of a civilization … I have said to the perfected steel, be my sister and for the glassy towers I thought I felt some beginnings of His creature, but *A,a,a, Domine Deus* …'[20] What is remarkable about Jones is that, beginning from the same absorption in

19. *Epoch and Artist*, p.299.
20. See the David Jones Special Issue of *Agenda* (1967), p.5. An earlier draft ends the essay on 'Art and sacrament' reprinted in *Epoch and Artist* (p.179).

Maritain as Gill,[21] he is able in both visual and verbal work to begin to frame some answers to the questions Gill so blithely ignores.

Jones' exposure to Maritain came through his participation in Gill's project. After demobilization in 1919, Jones studied first at the Westminster School of Art, where it appears that a Catholic friend introduced him to Fr John O'Connor. He became a Roman Catholic in 1921 and, prompted by O'Connor, joined Gill

21. See, for example, Jones's letter to Harman Grisewood in 1962: 'all this heterogeneous stuff given new point and cohesion by becoming a Catholic in 1921 and reading Maritain and meeting you and Tiger Dawson and Tom [Burns] and those various blokes we used to talk with in the late 1920s and early 1930s'. Rene Hague (ed.), *Dai Greatcoat. A Self-Portrait of David Jones in his Letters* (London: Faber, 1980), p.190, and cf. *Epoch and Artist*, p.172. An important guide to Maritain's influence on Jones can be found in Chapter 1 of Jonathan Miles, *Backgrounds to David Jones. A Study in Sources and Drafts* (Cardiff: University of Wales Press, 1990). See also Thomas Dilworth, 'David Jones and the Maritain conversation' in *David Jones: Diversity in Unity* (Cardiff: University of Wales Press, 2000), pp.43–55, an essay that rightly points out some of the ways in which Jones goes beyond Maritain.

at Ditchling later that year, moving in 1924 with the Gill family to Capel-y-ffin in Breconshire, then leaving for a spell at the monastery on Caldey Island; he was back in his native London in 1925, but returned to Capel and to Caldey for brief periods thereafter.[22] Thus he was alongside Gill and Gill's colleagues (he was for a time engaged to Gill's eldest daughter) during the crucial period during which they were all reading Maritain; and it is clear that for Jones – coming straight from a very different background – this made sense of what he had assimilated at the Westminster School of Art. He was to write much later (1971) that the basic insight of post-Impressionism had already implanted in him a sort of receptivity to sacramental theology – and to Maritain's understanding of art. 'The insistence that a painting must be a *thing* and not the impression of something has an affinity with what the Church said of the Mass.'[23]

22. Keith Alldritt's biography, *David Jones: Writer and Artist* (London: Constable, 2003), Chapters 6 and 7, is a good guide to his movements in this period.
23. Letter to Harman Grisewood, 1971, *Dai Greatcoat*, p.232. Cf. *Epoch and Artist*, pp.171–2.

But for Jones, the 'thinginess' of a product of art could not be, as for Gill, primarily or perhaps exclusively its firm and defined location in the geography of a theologically mapped culture. From the beginning, what preoccupies him is a set of problems about representation – not imitation or reproduction, but precisely what so concerns Maritain, the showing of the excess that pervades appearances. The artwork is indeed, as Gill put it, an extension of 'nature'; but it is so by the thoroughness of its transmutation of given nature into another material reality that reflects it and in so doing alters it and displays the hidden 'more than it is'. This helps to explain his commitment to watercolour and gouache; he is suspicious of the temptations of oils, so apt for the rendering of mass and depth. We have a few early attempts in this medium, but he largely forswears it after his first encounter with Gill.[24] Watercolour does not allow you to escape from two dimensions; it obliges you to translation or transubstantiation. The metaphor that Maritain uses so tellingly for the frustrated aspiration of a Rimbaud is here given

24. He exhibited an oil painting in the 1928 7 and 5 Exhibition (Alldritt, *op. cit.*, p.65).

a theologically reputable home in terms of an evocation of 'substance' that is related necessarily and inseparably but also ironically and multiply to material embodiment. Art shows that form is utterly bound to matter, yet also that this or that matter does not exhaust the possibilities of form. In the theological parallel Jones develops so richly in his essays, and to which we shall come back shortly, the substance of Christ's body is such that it is real only in the matter of the world – but no less intelligibly (even if more ambiguously) in the matter of the sacrament or the believing community than in the flesh that could be handled in Galilee. That flesh is more than it is, gives more than it (as flesh) has.

One generally helpful and nuanced discussion of Jones by Jonathan Miles has argued that the metaphor of transubstantiation is really misplaced, 'expressing something that is so much less than it suggests'.[25] Surely the product of art renders the 'qualities' of an object into the matter of art: 'No real magic occurs', whereas transubstantiation in the sacramental context *is* 'magical'. To assimilate it to the artistic process is actually to

25. Miles, *Backgrounds*, p.21.

61

reduce the sacramental claim to 'the Protestant idea of the significant relation between bread and body'.[26] The caution against taking the image uncritically is a useful one. But Jones is not, I think, talking about rendering *qualities* into other media; he is trying to make a larger claim. Something like the whole active presence of the object is being re-presented by the artist – not simply the *reproduction* of aspects of its appearance (since the artwork may not in fact be significantly concerned with reproducing 'qualities'). Jones would have taken perfectly seriously the philosophical and theological sense of participation between reality and representation that we have seen at work in Maritain; and this would certainly have given more weight to the metaphor than Miles allows. It is not that the sacramental is being reduced to the level of one discrete object 'signifying' another, but that the artistic work is being accorded a deeper metaphysical status. Without this background, the language is indeed weaker; but this looks forward to wider considerations about art and the character of existence itself, which we shall be looking at again in the last chapter of this study.

26. Ibid.

But all this illuminates what Jones has to say about the artist's 'double business', spelled out with great clarity in Jones's own notes written in 1935 for the Tate (later printed for the 1972 Kettle's Yard exhibition). He is describing what he takes to be a peculiarly Celtic dimension to what he is after – 'a certain affection for the intimate creatureliness of things – a care for, and appreciation of the particular genius of places, men, trees, animals, and yet withal a pervading sense of metamorphosis and mutability. That trees are men walking. That words "bind and loose" material things.'[27] This he associates with Welsh folklore, his lifelong passion, and, more surprisingly, with Lewis Carroll. But it is plain from this that he considers his task to be both a highly specific attention to what is given, and the need to 'thin out' the given materiality so as to re-embody what it is that is given and yet eludes the original embodiment.

The landscapes of the late 1920s show exactly what he meant. In the pieces painted during his time with Gill at Capel, and the years that

27. See Paul Hills' essay on Jones's art in the 1981 Tate Gallery catalogue, *David Jones*, pp.19–71; the text from the earlier catalogue is reproduced on pp.48–9.

immediately followed, we can see the rapid emergence of what has been called a 'sub-expressionist' style:[28] there are powerful linear patterns, a relentless 'verticality' – the depth of landscape transmuted into a sort of foreshortened perspective, the entire depth coming forward into the surface (as dramatically in 'The Waterfall, Afon Honddu Fach', 'Blaeau Bwch', 'Tir y Blaenau', the well-known 'Y Twympa', and – from his visit to Lourdes with the Gill family – 'Roman Land' and 'The River Gave in the Pyrenees'). The technique is already at work in pre-Capel works ('The Garden Enclosed', which uses an unusually dark palette and looks as though Jones has been absorbing a particular vein of Russian expressionism, Goncharova perhaps, or Larionov).[29] Nor is it only at work in landscape: 'The Suburban Order' (1926) and 'The Engraver's Workshop' (1929) are urban and domestic versions, the latter looking forward to the still-life work of

28. Miles, *Eric Gill and David Jones*, pp.140, 149.
29. These artists are distinguished by an affinity with primitivism (the folk art of Russian prints in particular) and some stirrings in the direction of cubism, an interest in formalized representation of volume, combined with a dense and dark coloration influenced by German expressionism.

the early 1930s. The 1931 'Place for Ships' brings together this crowded vertical pressure with the really remarkable work on the sea's colours and contours that he had refined on Caldey especially. And by this time his palette has become magnificently distinctive. As Paul Hills argued in his excellent Tate catalogue of 1981, Jones's habit of not painting regularly in a steady north light but frequently with the light in his face meant that 'academic tonal relationships are confounded: an object in the distance silhouetted against a bright light – a steamer against the sea – may appear darker than anything closer to the eye'.[30] His use of gouache in some of the late 1920s paintings allows him, again as Hills notes, to achieve some of the effects of oil (the visibility of brushwork, for example) without letting go of his absolute commitment to the flat surface of the watercolour.[31] And his use of pencil line intensifies this commitment to the eye working on a surface.

In the late 1920s and early 1930s, he was close to figures like the Nicholsons and Christopher Wood; there are elements that drift towards

30. Hills, *op.cit.*, p.47.
31. Ibid., p.37.

Fauvism or even surrealism.[32] He was manifestly in the mainstream of the modern movement in British visual art; from 1928, he was a member of the influential 7 and 5 Group, and exhibited with them (showing in 1928 one of his very few oils from this period). But the nervous illness that overtook him in 1932 changed things permanently. He had begun to work on his first poetic enterprise; and his visual production shifts towards what some have (wrongly) thought a more dematerialized style.[33] There are landscapes and still lifes as before; but the work moves towards the intensely symbolic vein that most associate with his work. What is completely continuous

32. Miles, *Eric Gill and David Jones*, Chapter 10; cf. Hills, *op. cit.*, p.48.

33. Jonathan Miles and Derek Shiel, *David Jones: The Maker Unmade* (Bridgend: Seren Books, 1995) argue that the visual work of the later period is pervasively over-intellectualized and, so to speak, de-sensualized. This is ascribed to Jones's failure to resolve tensions around sexuality and religious commitment, a failure also evidenced in his ever more mythologized treatment of the female face or form. I think that this underrates the continuities in the work; granted the struggle with over-elaboration evident in some later work (like the notorious 'A Latere Dextro'), the concern with the paradox of the representative surface remains.

with what went before is the vertical and linear emphasis. But what he now brings out by this is what is best seen as an effect of multiple exposure in the visual image: linear designs are superimposed, they intersect or simply coexist on a surface where pigment is minimal. 'The Farm Door' of 1937 is probably the first really distinctive essay in this vein, but it develops through the extraordinary 'Aphrodite in Aulis' (finished in 1941) and 'Vexilla Regis' (1948) to the wonderful chalice paintings of 1950 and 1951 (I am surprised to find these described as merely 'charming' in Alldritt's recent biography)[34] and finally the masterpieces of the early 1960s, 'Trystan ac Essyllt' and 'Y Cyfarchiad i Fair' ('The Annunciation'), this last one of his best-known images, appropriately uniting the dense allusiveness of his mature literary work with the Welsh hill landscape that had absorbed him nearly four decades earlier.

Much has been written about the detail of pictures like the 'Cyfarchiad';[35] but I am concerned

34. Alldritt, *op.cit.*, p.145.
35. A good discussion is that by Arthur Giardelli, 'Three related works by David Jones' in the second (1974) David Jones Special Issue of *Agenda*, pp.90–8, especially pp.94ff.

here with what his actual technique says about the perspective underlying the work. As in the chalice paintings (especially 'Flora in Calix-Light'), the pencil lines, very delicate and exact, present superimposed layers of representation. In the 'Cyfarchiad', we have to look at the detail of the flowers and the bird life, and the woven hedge, all drawn with what Kenneth Clark called 'the skill and precision of a de Limbourg';[36] but this is not a reproduction of anything, so the 'realism' is in one sense beside the point. Or rather, its point is in its absolute refusal to be anything other than linear, so that further detail can be interwoven or posed in tension with it. This is how you show what is 'more than it is': the birds are not a naturalistic or even symbolic-naturalistic background for Mary's spiritual encounter as they might be in a mediaeval (Limbourg) or pre-Raphaelite depiction; they are the mobile life of an actual landscape that is being 're-lit' by the non-local but utterly concrete presence of the coming of the Word of God. They are a visual transcription of Jones's ever-deepening preoccupation with the image of the land itself as 'The

36. Kenneth Clark, 'Some recent paintings of David Jones', in the 1967 *Agenda* (pp.97–100), p.99.

Sleeping Lord', the immanent and imminent presence of God's meanings, pregnant in the local and immediate.[37] At this level, there is no real difference between this explicitly religious picture and 'Flora in Calix-Light'. This is how you paint 'excess': by the delicate superimposing of nets of visual material in a way that teases constantly by simultaneously refusing a third dimension and insisting that there is no way of reading the one surface at once. As in the Byzantine icon, visual depth gives way to the time taken to 'read' a surface: you cannot construct a single consistent illusion of depth as you look, and so you are obliged to trace and re-trace the intersecting linear patterns.

37. See 'The sleeping lord', *Agenda* 1967, pp.28–54, and the longer collection under the same title (London: Faber, 1974).

3

Paul Hills quotes from a letter of 1952 to Fr Desmond Chute in which Jones very tellingly compares his technique as a visual artist with what he was attempting in his written work: 'I find, or think I find, the process almost identical', he says.[38] And ten years later he writes to Harman Grisewood about the difficulty many critics experienced in placing him as a poet: 'all I tried to do was to see how the business of "form" and "content" worked in writing in relation to what I knew of how it worked in drawing'.[39] A much earlier note on this, written for his doctor in 1947, explains that in painting 'one is led partly by what evolves as the painting evolves, this form suggesting that form – happiness comes when the forms assume significance with regard

38. Hills, *op. cit.*, p.44. Derek Shiels, 'David Jones the maker', David Jones Special Issue of the *Chesterton Review* (vol. xxiii, 1–2, 1997, pp.157–63), cautions against too facile a reading of this sort of identification on the grounds of Jones's failure to embody tragedy or irony in his visual art as he does in his poetry. This is arguable; but the connection in *method* remains significant in any case.

39. *Dai Greatcoat*, p.189.

to this juxtaposition with each other – even though the original "idea" was somewhat different'.[40] He is again taking Maritain a stage further: the half-apprehended consonance of impressions out of which an artwork grows has to be realized in the process of actually creating significant forms which, in the process of their embodiment, in stone, words, or pigment, uncover other resonances, so that what finally emerges is more than just a setting down of what was first grasped.

In Jones's poetry, this makes for a density that can, by common consent, be alarming. To read *In Parenthesis* adequately, you have to have a level of alertness to the concrete reality of the trenches in 1916 or thereabouts, to a British military history behind that, to the Trojan war, the Arthurian cycles and the liturgy of the Passion. The famous frontispiece and tailpiece to the work set the tone: the frontispiece, with its naked soldier pulling on an army jacket against a background of splintered trees, with (a favourite motif) a horse in the distance grazing under a tree, makes the soldier in the trenches a kind of Adam, half-naked, half-clothed, ensnared in the

40. Ibid., p.137.

trees; and, as Paul Hills suggests, a Christ 'putting on' human nature.[41] The riderless horse is an Arthurian motif, echoed in his great *Vexilla Regis* (as he explained to Helen Ede).[42] The tailpiece is unambiguously the slaughtered Lamb, caught in the thicket of barbed wire, again with a background of broken or lopped trees. Throughout the work, the texture of the words translates the pictorial technique – intersecting and crisscrossing lines on a surface, realities superimposed; the bleakness of the trenches both being and 'giving' a history of futile slaughter and heroism, and equally opening up a simple and direct light into some foundational truth about sacrifice and freedom, looking back to Abraham and Isaac and supremely to the event that the Mass makes present. There are passages that chillingly underscore the impersonal character of the warfare of 1916 and of the mass death it generates – a well-known few lines depict the marching soldiers as 'wired dolls' jerking mechanically against the sky.[43]

41. Hills, *op.cit.*, pp.58–9.
42. *Dai Greatcoat*, p.150.
43. *In Parenthesis*, London, Faber, 1937, p.37. Hills (*op. cit.*, p.22) notes that this is a description 'in terms of the syntax of Cubism, not only its dehumanized geometry but also its synthetic, dramatic lighting'.

But this is set in counterpoint to the haunting imagery of sheep going to the slaughter, which opens up that mechanical vision to the sacrifice of Christ. And the folkloric section in Part 7 where the dead soldiers are crowned by the Queen of the Woods ('Some she gives white berries/ some she gives brown … Hansel with Gronwy share dog-violets for palm, where they lie in serious embrace beneath the twisted tripod')[44] offers a perspective on the casual and brutal deaths endured by ordinary soldiers that is hard to reduce either to consolatory religious language or to a merely decorative mythology. It is simply that something completely outside the framework of prose and history establishes – to pick up one of the most striking words here – seriousness about the human loss. And the angry irony of some passages about sentimental celebration of such loss allows Jones to bring into relief the only celebration that actually respects and heals. 'Give them glass eyes to see and synthetic spare parts to walk in the Triumphs, without anyone feeling awkward and O, O, O, it's a lovely war with poppies on the up-platform for a perpetual memorial of his body.'[45]

44. Ibid., pp.185–6.
45. Ibid., p.176.

There is much more to be said about the way in which *In Parenthesis* prepares the way for later fragments inviting us to see the events of Christ's passion through the eyes of Roman soldiers (some of them auxiliary recruits from Britain) serving in Jerusalem.[46] Rome, the Celtic world, modern imperialisms, the Latin of the Mass and the offices – all are brought together in one complex verbal 'surface' covered with interlacing lines. But if there is a point of convergence, a centre to the knot-work, it is the cross itself. And this is equally what is at work in the most sophisticated and 'achieved' work of Jones' maturity, the *Anathemata*. The introduction to this particular thicket of allusion develops that very image, the hunt in the thicket; picking up from the Dominican theologian Thomas Gilby's description of the mind as 'hunter of forms'[47] (echoed in a well-known poem of Geoffrey Hill's, incidentally, or not so incidentally),[48]

46. See *The Roman Quarry and Other Sequences*, ed. Harman Grisewood (London: Agenda Editions, 1981).
47. Jones quotes this in the Preface to the *Anathemata* (London: Faber, 1952), p.19; also reprinted in *Epoch and Artist*, p.116.
48. Geoffrey Hill, *Tenebrae* (London: Andre Deutsch, 1978), p.19 ('Self-seeking hunter of forms, there is no end/to such pursuits.')

Jones lays out the process of searching for poetic form as a search for the complex of inter-reference that makes up the cultural identity of the poet herself.[49] It is a hunt for what makes the poet's mind possible; and as the work unfolds, this definition takes on a double aspect. At the more obvious level, it is about what makes *this* poet's mind possible, the cultural specifics of a London Welshman 'of Protestant upbringing, of Catholic subscription'.[50] But then it is also and more importantly about what makes *any* poet possible: the ontology, if we can use that forbidding word here, of a universe that is inextricably both material and significative, where things matter intensely, but matter in ways that breach boundaries and carry significance beyond what they tangibly are. Words are material communication; things are material words. And the distinctive fact about humanity is this double business, as I have already called it, of attention to the creaturely and immediate, and involvement, known or unknown, in the making of meaning or the uncovering of connection.[51] In this

49. Preface to the *Anathemata*, pp.19–20 (*Epoch and Artist*, pp.116–17).
50. Ibid., p.11 (*Epoch and Artist*, p.109).
51. Ibid., p.33 (*Epoch and Artist*, p.129).

context, the poet is exhibiting the human as such, not in what is written but in the act of writing like this.

But the human as such is always located, rooted, so that the second aspect of what makes the poet's mind possible is never without the first. Hence, Jones is clear that he begins with the specific tracks of association that are realized in one highly particular setting – his own participation in the Roman liturgy. The *Anathemata* is set in the course of the Mass, which is for Jones the place where the meaning of meaning is displayed; displayed in the history that the Mass celebrates and makes contemporary, displayed in the chains of allusion and connection that occur in this person's awareness or half-awareness as the rite proceeds.[52] You have to start somewhere; and Jones's argument in the introduction notes the ways in which the modern imagination is radically deprived of most of what made the world of signs possible, natural and intelligible in the past, before the great 'Break' of the modern age.[53] The sense of ontological depth to metaphor,

52. Ibid., pp.31–2 (*Epoch and Artist*, pp.127–8).
53. Ibid., pp.22–3 (*Epoch and Artist*, pp.119–20).

the awareness of participatory patterns under the surface of appearance so that thinking itself is always allusive and (in every sense) involved – this has shrunk dramatically, and to write in such a way as to display what the act of imaginative writing itself *is* becomes a challenge. 'It is precisely this validity and availability [of images] that constitutes [the artist's] greatest problem in the present culture situation.'[54] Where is the poet to start today, if she is to show what is foundationally human? If the poet is fortunate enough to have access to one of the few contexts left in which *anamnesis*, ritual recollection in word and rite, occurs, where else should she start?

The modern artist in general, though, does not know where she is; and if you do not know where you are, you cannot easily 'lift up signs', in Jones's phrase. If you cannot place a perception, a specific thing, in the context of its resonances and formal echoes, you cannot place it at all. As a matter of fact, because artists know more than they think they know, they continually *do* 'place' percepts and things in these ways. But making sense of what this is has become

54. Ibid., p.23 (*Epoch and Artist*, p.120).

obscure. Someone has to locate his poetry more openly in relation to what makes significance occur. And so the work begins with the priest at the altar: 'We already and first of all discern him making this thing other'[55] – literally where the *Anathemata* starts. The first section of the poem evokes the history and prehistory of making signs, the history of the creature who is called *sapiens*, a mind capable of *sapientia*, a mind that can speak, a body that can dance in ritual, a perception that can make one thing another in word or picture. The constant refrain of these pages is the question 'How else?' Without this human history, how could there be a priest at the altar re-presenting in another form an act (the self-surrender of the incarnate divine Word, the divine connection of meaning) that supremely communicates to the material world the transformative liberty of God. It is God who makes meanings because it is God, speaker of the eternal Word who becomes flesh, who connects finite reality with the communicative, the self-imparting, action that is divine life.

The *Anathemata* moves on through an often bewildering world of Roman and post-Roman

55. Ibid., p.49.

Britain, the Arthurian legend in both its early Welsh form and its mature expression in Malory, the archaeology of London, British naval history, a wide reference to English folksong and folklore and a good deal besides, littered with Welsh, both early and modern, Latin and a bit of Greek. Quotation is difficult; but there are parts of Section VI that bring out especially plainly some of the depth of reference. The title of this section is 'Keel, Ram, Stauros'; growing out of the previous sections that deal with London and the sea traffic coming in to the port, we begin with the ship's keel, 'the trembling tree ... the quivering elm on which our salvation sways ... Yardstick, prime measure'.[56] Like the great world-tree that is also the cross in Jones's 'Vexilla Regis' painting, the keel-timber begins 'forechosen and ringed/in the dark arbour-lands'.[57] But such a timber might equally be a battering-ram, blessed by a Roman priest as the siege is laid to a city with words from the archaic hymn to Mars urging the god to 'leap the *limes*', jump over the boundary.[58] Or simply a wayside cross: neglected, sometimes

56. Ibid., p.173.
57. Ibid., p.175.
58. Ibid., p.176.

deliberately defaced or ignored when people turn to other saviours, but standing among faded flowers and candles.[59] And then this section of the poem swings back to the ship, the hidden keel soaked with the refuse of the ship as its master brings her to shore: 'He would berth us/ to schedule'.[60]

This gives little idea of the Joycean inventiveness of the wordplay, the verbal nudges and half-echoes, of this section alone. But the 'schedule' – and the punning 'berth' – of the last line begins to bring the heavy ship of the whole composition back towards the calendar of Christian mythology; Section VII is a Midnight Mass in post-Roman Britain, locating the narrative of the mother and child against the classical background of spirits and sybils and the Celtic myths of divine and heroic children and their goddess mothers. And the final movement of the work takes us to Maundy Thursday and Good Friday; to the taking of bread at the Last Supper and the crucial, axial exchange between God and the world on the cross. The Mass reaches its climax,

59. Ibid., pp.178–9.
60. Ibid., p.182.

the words are spoken and the bread lifted up, a material sign of a material sign, a sacrament of the ultimately sacramental humanity of Christ.

> What did he do other
>   recumbent at the garnished supper?
> What did he do yet other
>   Riding the Axile Tree?[61]

61. Ibid., p.243.

4

Art is an uncovering of what is uniquely human; and what is uniquely human depends in some way that defies exact statement on those connections that are held and sustained by whatever and whoever it is that is incarnate in Christ: that human life that is most supremely charged with significance (because it speaks for the maker of all things) becomes a sign, a material word, lets itself be taken into the world of sign-making and communication by means of the institution of the Mass; and so to take your stand in the context of the Mass is to be where sign-making is grounded or vindicated. Jones's indebtedness to the Jesuit theologian Maurice de la Taille's discussion of the Eucharist is a pervasive feature of his work; de la Taille gives him a formula for a wide range of imaginative labour when he describes Christ at the Last Supper 'placing himself in the order of signs'.[62] God makes himself other; the world is a world in which things make themselves other or are made other (they are more than they are and give more than they have); human beings are those creatures who uniquely have the capacity and responsibility to uncover for one another the

nature of the world in which sameness and otherness constantly flow into each other, and in which
there is no final reading of a 'surface', whether
the literal surface of a sheet of paper or the surface, the first perception, of a narrative, a song, an
action. Jones's practice as poet and visual artist
displays all this with extraordinary energy and
depth. But in the mid-1950s he summarized his
vision in a single essay which not only illuminates his work overall but also suggests where he
used Maritain's categories to go beyond Maritain.

62. 'He placed himself in the order of signs' is the title page
epigraph to *Epoch and Artist*, and the same quotation
concludes the essay on 'Art and sacrament'. De la Taille's
work, *Mysterium Fidei*, first appeared in Latin in 1924,
and an English epitome was published, along with other
pieces by the same author, in 1930 (*The Mystery of Faith
and Human Opinion Contrasted and Defined* (London:
Sheed and Ward). On de la Taille's impact on Jones, see
the introductory remarks to the printing of his précis of
Mysterium Fidei in the *Chesterton Review*, 1997, pp.127ff.,
and the brief but perceptive comment by Jenifer M. Dye,
'David Jones: artist, writer, theologian?' in the same issue,
pp.135–7. Towards the end of his life, Jones was pleased
to know that de la Taille's reputation had revived in some
theological circles (William Blissett, *The Long Conversation.
A Memoir of David Jones* (Oxford University Press, 1981),
pp. 75, 93, 115).

'Art and Sacrament' was published in 1955, as one
of a collection of essays dealing with the 'Catholic' attitude to various areas of contemporary
life and work.[63] It begins by taking us back to
the distinction that had now become canonical
in so much Catholic writing on aesthetics between art and prudence; but Jones refuses to take
the familiar terms of the distinction wholly for
granted. He notes – as others hadn't – that the
two terms are not self-evidently comparable: art
is an activity, prudence a quality *of* an activity. It
does not greatly help to argue about their spheres
of operation or their relative importance. Go
back to even more basic principles, and you can
see that prudence is pervasive in human self-
understanding: even if you abandon the ethics
of revealed religion, issues of better and worse,
wiser and more foolish, realistic and unrealistic,
shoulds and shouldn'ts are unavoidable in anything we'd call a human life. We are beings who
have choices about these things, and we can't
avoid involvement in them; we reason about our
situation and shape our acts accordingly. In
brief, we are free; we do things because we have

63. *Catholic Approaches* (London: Weidenfeld and
    Nicolson, 1955); pp.143–79 in *Epoch and Artist*.

reflected and come to a policy, not because we set out to meet a simple cluster of needs. There is an 'intransitive' element in us, a habit of doing things that have significance. We choose because an act has potential meaning for us or others, not because we are bound to exercise these specific functions.[64]

So 'in the very process of somewhat tortuously considering why man (if he exists) is a creature of faith and morals and is thus the darling of Prudentia, we find ourselves unexpectedly confronted, as by an old friend at a street's bend, with man's natural activity, the activity we call "art"'.[65] Prudence is to do with how we make lives significant, not about how we meet our needs; so art is a necessary accompaniment of prudence. 'There is a common cause preventing the animals from being either prudential beings or artists.'[66] Animals (the ant, the spider, the nuthatch) produce work of outstanding beauty, but it is like the beauty of the natural world because it is 'transitive', it has a definable and

64. *Epoch and Artist*, pp.145–51.
65. Ibid., pp.148–9.
66. Ibid., p.150.

general function; human activity aims at the embodying of meaning by deliberate choices, and this gratuitous element in what is human makes the difference between us and other creatures. It is, Jones further suggests, something to do with the fact that, for Christian theology, God's act of creation is utterly gratuitous, describable as a kind of play.[67]

The essay proceeds to argue that the whole notion of *sign* implies the sacred – the real as good, the good as supremely real, and thus as laying on us an obligation, a binding. If the stuff of the world can be a medium of communication, the exploration of the possible meanings of what is given becomes a listening for something like a gift, the bestowing on us of a share in a reality that is for our flourishing. So we are bound to undertake 'judgement' in the conduct of our specifically human business, discrimination, as we seek new forms or new collocations of forms. As we select and shape our forms – whether in poetry, painting or military strategy (Jones's deliberately unexpected example here)[68] – we seek to bind

67. Ibid., pp.153–4.
68. Ibid., pp.159–61; cf. the essay on 'Art in Relation to War'.

ourselves by the exercise of judgement to what
is, because of a conviction that the real (when
finally discerned or uncovered) is good.

'Some man known to the reader may indeed
appear to escape from all that is commonly or
vulgarly meant by the "sacramental", but no
sooner does he put a rose in his buttonhole but
what he is already in the trip-wire of sign.'[69] As
the union of material being and meaningful
imagination, humanity alone has the gift of
sign-making, and humanity alone cannot avoid
sign-making. Without this recognition, we fail
to understand the nature of sacramental action;
equally though, sacramental action is the
supreme illumination of what and who we are,
and art fails to understand itself without sacramental reference. Jones again refers to his formative experience as an art student in 1919, the
discovery that what the post-Impressionists
were saying about making something other was
most clearly evident in the Mass. In this brief
'autobiographical digression' in the essay, Jones
recalls how Maritain's work offered at that time
an exhilarating perspective on the idea that art

69. Ibid., p.167.

was fundamentally *making* – not copying, not free-wheeling or expressing an inner selfhood, but producing a material thing.[70] Yet the whole of this remarkable essay of Jones's, one of the most important pieces of writing in the twentieth century on art and the sacred, illustrates a point Maritain does not quite get to. Jones implies that the life of 'prudence', a life lived in a con-sciously moral context, however exactly under-stood, is itself an act of gratuitous sign-making; moral behaviour is the construction of a life that can be 'read', that reveals something in the world and uncovers mystery. It is not something that Jones develops systematically, but it foreshadows a good deal of writing about religious ethics in more recent years – what we have learned to call 'virtue ethics' and 'narrative ethics', and ethics ex-plicitly rooted in communal practices of meaning.[71]

70. Cf. n.23 above.
71. This is a trend especially associated with the work of Alasdair MacIntyre (in his work from *After Virtue* (London: Duckworth, 1981) onwards). Possible par-allels between Jones and MacIntyre are explored by A. C. Everatt, 'Doing and making' in Belinda Humfrey and Anne Price-Owen (eds), *David Jones: Diversity in Unity* (Cardiff: University of Wales Press, 2000), pp.65–74.

Almost without noticing, he has turned away from both legalism and subjectivism in morality and opened up a new and tantalizing perspective on behaviour as a kind of art, a search for forms that will uncover the interconnectedness of reality.

But this point about the way in which a life may become a significant form – as, decisively and uniquely, in the life of Christ – also leads us towards a new set of questions about the creative arts. Jones was a visual artist and poet; these are the arts that Maritain has most to say about. What about the art in which narrative and character predominate? Maritain has surprisingly little to say about drama, and his interventions in debate about fiction were not productive of anything much except a monumental quarrel with Georges Bernanos.[72] But Jones's ruminations on the gratuitous element in prudence prompt us to ask how a Maritainian theory of art would look applied to the creation of story and character, the re-presenting of a life that signifies. In the next chapter, my subject will be a writer for whom these were the pressing practical issues. Jones's

72. See Ralph McInerny, *The Very Rich Hours of Jacques Maritain*, pp.107–8.

clear theological agenda – the impossibility of grasping the human centrality of art without some awareness of a 'binding' (*religio*) to unseen continuities held in intelligible harmony by the divine Word – will need some further exploration in the fourth chapter. He undertakes his work consistently in the faith that it is, simply *as* the kind of labour it is, a showing of something fundamental, as well as an enterprise constantly being drawn back to one specific narrative, the Word become sign in the events of the Last Supper and the Passion. It is a faith consistently tested to the extreme of failure and frustration, especially as he grows older: there is too much to say and the forms slip and elude. Yet he will hold to the belief that 'There is only one tale to tell even though the telling is patient of endless development and ingenuity and can take on a million different forms. I imagine something of this sort to be implicit in what Picasso is reported as saying: "I do not seek, I find."'[73]

73. *Epoch and Artist*, p.130 (cf. pp.98–9.)

THREE

Flannery O'Connor: Proper Names

In 1957, Mary Flannery O'Connor sent a copy of *Art and Scholasticism* to a friend, describing it as 'the book I cut my aesthetic teeth on, though I think even some of the things he says get soft at times'.[1] 'Soft' may be an odd word to use of Maritain (I shall be trying later to suggest why she uses it), but it is certainly a word no one would readily use of O'Connor herself. Her letters and essays, like her fiction, reflect an uncompromising intellect, unfashionable, sceptical and satirical, almost destructive; most of her adult life was spent at her mother's home in rural Georgia, since the onset of lupus, which killed her at the age of

1. Flannery O'Connor, *The Habit of Being. Letters Edited with an Introduction by Sally Fitzgerald* (New York: Farrar, Strauss and Giroux, 1979) (henceforth HB), p.216. She was not alone among American literary figures in her appreciation: Allen and Caroline (Gordon) Tate, who were friends and allies of hers, shared her interest (see *Exiles and Fugitives: The Letters of Jacques and Raissa Maritain, Allen Tate and Caroline Gordon* (Louisiana State University Press, 1993)). On these connections between Catholic thought and literary movements in the American South in the mid-twentieth century, there is a great deal of material in Francesca Aran Murphy's excellent *Christ the Form of Beauty: A Study in Theology and Literature* (Edinburgh: T. and T. Clark, 1995).

39, had prevented her living alone, and she had decided to return to her roots. Her involvement with the respectable society of Milledgeville, as chronicled in her letters, was a constant exercise in irony, sometimes benevolent, sometimes less so.[2] A cradle Catholic, unlike Maritain and David Jones, she was a robust defender of orthodox doctrine and traditional devotion, as well as being a scathing critic of religious subculture. Some of her most pungent observations are to do with assumptions about 'Catholic art' that insist that such art should be edifying and moral; this, she argues, plays straight into the hands of critics of the Church who hold that dogmatic belief incapacitates a creative writer. On the contrary: 'The Catholic writer, insofar as he has the mind of the Church, will feel life from the standpoint of the central Christian mystery: that it has, for all its horror, been found by God to be worth dying for.'[3]

2. For biographical information, see Harold Fickett and Douglas R. Gilbert, *Flannery O'Connor: Images of Grace* (Grand Rapids: Eerdmans, 1986), and Paul Elie, *The Life You Save May Be Your Own. An American Pilgrimage* (New York: Farrar, Strauss and Giroux, 2003) (a comparative study of O'Connor, Walker Percy, Dorothy Day and Thomas Merton).

3. Flannery O' Connor, *Mystery and Manners. Occasional Prose* (London: Faber, 1972) (henceforth MM), p.146.

And this means that the Catholic writer is precisely someone who cannot rule out any subject matter; belief adds a dimension to what is seen, it does not take anything away.[4] 'The Catholic fiction writer is entirely free to observe. He feels no call to take on the duties of God or to create a new universe ... He feels no need to apologize for the ways of God to man or to avoid looking at the ways of man to God.'[5] This imposes on the Catholic writer a dangerous task, since she has to deal with matters that may indeed be 'occasions of sin', subjects that expose the worst in humanity. And while 'to look at the worst will be for [the writer] no more than an act of trust in God',[6] it may be a source of danger for the reader.

This can be a paralysing prospect, a Medusa that turns the writer to stone, in O'Connor's forceful image.[7] It can only be dealt with by the asceticism that concentrates on what is actually to be done, the logic and integrity of the work to be made. To ask about possible moral consequences

4. MM, p.150.
5. MM, p.178.
6. MM, p.148.
7. MM, p.187.

is to interrupt this integrity. But the paradoxical point is that if the writer urgently wants to lay bare a moral universe or a dogmatic structure, she has to do so exclusively in the terms of the work itself, not by introducing a moral excursus or by holding back because of possible undesirable results in a vulnerable reader. Of course, she would say, the work is 'propagandist' in the sense that it claims truthful vision and seeks to recreate that vision in the reader; but it must do this by not interfering in what is seen. Belief, remember, adds to vision and does not subtract; the plausibility of a work of fiction dealing with humanity's relation to God is inseparable from its refusal to make easy or tidy up the data of a world that is recognizable to anyone not sharing the writer's specific commitments. On this, it is worth quoting her at length:

'This means that [the work] must carry its meaning inside it. It means that any abstractly expressed compassion or piety or morality in a piece of fiction is only a statement added to it. It means that you can't make an inadequate dramatic action complete by putting a statement of meaning on the end of it or in the middle of it or at the beginning of it. It means that when you write fiction you are speaking *with* character and action, not *about* character and action.'[8]

Here is her clearest statement of what Maritain's aesthetic means applied to fiction; and one of its interesting corollaries is a parallel point to the one that Maritain himself makes about how modern poetry reveals something essential to the poetic craft that classical models can conceal. The retreat in much contemporary fiction of the presence of a supposedly neutral or omniscient narrator focuses us more directly on the actual task of fiction. In an important sense, the narrator must not 'speak'; the action and the character must. Or, to develop O'Connor's point somewhat, a narrator within a fiction must be precisely that – *within* the fiction, a clearly *fictional* narrator, a character among characters. Thus action and character must have the realized life, the wholeness, that the process of the work demands. Self-expression is ruled out; what matters is the search for the internal *necessity* of a work. 'Strangle that word *dreams*', she wrote to the friend to whom she had sent Maritain; 'You don't dream

8.   MM, pp.75–6.

up a form and put the truth in it. The truth creates its own form. Form is necessity in the work of art. You know what you mean but you ain't got the right words for it.'[9] In a lecture on 'The Nature and Aim of Fiction', she quotes Aquinas on art as 'reason in making', glossing this as meaning that for the artist 'to be reasonable is to find, in the object, in the situation, in the sequence, the spirit which makes it itself'.[10] And because 'dogma is an instrument for penetrating reality',[11] religious belief should be an aid to 'reason in making' – that is, to the discernment of what truly *is* in the environment so that this active content can be understood as it is re-embodied in the artist's labour. The dogma does not dictate the shape of the narrative but enables the proper action of

9. HB, p.218; cf. e.g. MM, pp.153, 162. And her view of writing courses encouraging self-expression is memorably summarized in a lecture on the nature of fiction: 'Everywhere I go I'm asked if I think the universities stifle writers. My opinion is that they don't stifle enough of them ... The idea of being a writer attracts a good many shiftless people, those who are merely burdened with poetic feelings or afflicted with sensibility.' (MM, pp.84–5.)
10. MM, p.82.
11. MM, p.178.

narrating to take place – very much as, for David Jones, the act of poetic labour is itself theologically charged.

So: the fiction writer is out to 'do justice' to the world, in a phrase of Conrad's that O'Connor obviously liked;[12] but 'to believe nothing is to see nothing',[13] and every artist, like it or not, works with a framework of assumptions about humanity and its world.[14] The visible appearances that are the indispensable building blocks of the writer's work are already organized in this way or that; and the claim of Catholic doctrine is that it offers the most comprehensive, least selective way of reading the world that could be imagined because it identifies the real finally with the good (a point we have seen in David Jones), in the strongest possible sense – the sense for which the good must be the loveable, or perhaps is good because it is loved. Doing justice to the visible world is reflecting the love of God for it, the fact that this world is worth dying for in God's eyes. The tightrope that the Catholic writer must walk

12. The quotation appears in HB, p.128, and MM, pp.80, 157.
13. HB, p.147.
14. See, e.g., MM, p.91.

is to forget or ignore nothing of the visually, morally, humanly sordid world, making nothing easy for the reader, while doing so in the name of a radical conviction that sees that world being interrupted and transfigured by revelation. The event that disrupts and questions and changes the world is precisely what obliges the artist not to try and recreate it from scratch. Irony is going to be unavoidable in this exercise.

It is not a word we have encountered much so far in this discussion. For O'Connor, the artist takes the risk of uncovering the world within the world of visible things as a way of 'doing justice', confident because of her commitment that what is uncovered will be the 'reason' in things, a consonance that is well beyond any felt harmony or system of explanation but is simply a coherence and connectedness always more than can be seen or expressed. Because of this trust, she can push towards the limits of what is thinkable and 'acceptable', let alone edifying. She is always taking for granted that God is possible – thinkable or accessible or even manifest – in the most grotesque and empty or cruel situations; she pursues the unacceptable in the ironic faith that the pursuit will vindicate God, at least to the extent that God is intrinsic to whatever is uncovered in the work of writing. It is a sort of transcription of George Herbert's poetic technique of licensing more and more violent expressions of rebellion in the confidence that they will be halted and absorbed in the divine word that interrupts;[15] but the irony is deeper because here you have to imagine voices and histories other than your own in which God's freedom must be lured into appearing by testing the moral limits of a situation.

What's more, in a cultural environment where grace is not part of an expected or understood landscape, it is only by such extreme irony that grace can be made to be 'natural'. She is, as critics have repeatedly observed, writing as a Catholic in a culturally deeply Protestant situation, and part of her objection to cultural Protestantism is that it fails to make grace perceptible or credible in its practice; hence her concentration on the wilder reaches of Protestantism, the lonely prophets and

15. Cf. Rowan Williams, *Anglican Identities* (London: Darton, Longman and Todd, 2003), pp.57–72, on George Herbert; also Elizabeth Clarke, *Theory and Theology in George Herbert's Poetry: 'Divinitie and Poesy, Met'* (Oxford: Clarendon Press, 1997).

madmen who somehow know the reality of grace
and invent a kind of sacramentalism of their own.
The mixture in her environment of bourgeois
Protestant respectability and the pervasive under-
current of an untamed and often dangerous reli-
giosity serves her well.[16] 'You have to make your
vision apparent by shock' says O'Connor,[17] given
that 'the supernatural is an embarrassment today
even to many of the churches'.[18]

The 'supernatural' here does not of course mean
the paranormal, but the action of God, perceived
as it touches the human condition in ways that
open up a radically 'other' depth in things. It is
both deeply strange to the created order, which
can get along without it for practical purposes or,
rather, thinks it can (a good neo-Thomist point),
yet also familiar and usual, that on to which the

16. Ralph C. Wood, *Flannery O'Connor and the Christ-
    Haunted South* (Grand Rapids: Eerdmans, 2004), is a
    helpful collection of essays on this point, especially
    Chapters 1, 4 and 5.
17. MM, p.34, cf. p.185.
18. MM, p.163. This aspect of O'Connor's work is dis-
    cussed very perceptively in D. Z. Phillips, *Faith After
    Foundationalism. Critiques and Alternatives* (London:
    Routledge, 1988), Chapter 22.

ordinary constantly opens. So the Catholic writer of fiction must offer a recognizable world that is also utterly unexpected – just as we noted with David Jones the tension between 'an affection for the intimate creatureliness of things' and the metamorphosis that somehow recognizes the excess in things, their giving of themselves for surplus significance and meaning.[19] Translated into the fiction writer's terms, this means that the Catholic novelist like O'Connor has to create agents in fiction who embody excess of meaning, and whose relations with each other and with the usually hidden otherness of God are not limited by the visible, though they are inconceivable without the visible. The uncompromising specificity of the dogma of the Incarnation and the action of the Mass again becomes a key to the artist's task: the infinite cannot be *directly* apprehended, so we must take appearance seriously; it is the *infinite* that is being apprehended, so we must take appearance seriously enough to read its concealments and stratagems: 'He's tricked me before with his manifold lurking places.'[20]

19. Above, p.63.
20. MM, p.163. The final phrase is from Jones, 'A, domine Deus'.

'The prophet is a realist of distances, and it is this kind of realism that goes into great novels.'[21] A realist of distances, like David Jones painting objects as dark against a bright sky shining in his face, or making a landscape's contour into a complex surface, creates details, creates figures that seem unreal if we stand too close, yet whose words and acts and interrelations emerge as uncovering, deciphering, the real substructure of the whole human landscape. This illuminates also what O'Connor says about what she thinks makes a story work as a story – 'some action, some gesture of a character that is unlike any other in the story, one which indicates where the real heart of the story lies ... both totally right and totally unexpected ... both in character and beyond character; it would have to suggest both time and eternity'.[22] It would be an act that, theologically, represented our participation in God's action by embodying gratuity and excess; but not an allegory of divine action or a moral lesson. Thus the pivotal point of a fiction is a moment when the irony is most intense; it is not that the finite rises without interruption to a degree of

21. MM, p.179.
22. MM, p.111.

sublimity but that the actuality of grace is uncovered in the moment of excess – which may
be in a deliberately intensified gracelessness –
without doing violence to the narrative surface.

2

What exactly does she mean? She herself refers to her well-known and much anthologized story, 'A Good Man is Hard to Find',[23] which describes a tediously squabbling family on an outing that ends in horror. They get lost, the car turns over in a ditch, and the first vehicle to stop in this desolate setting contains an escaped convict, a psychopathic murderer. Quietly and purposefully, he and his companions kill the family one by one; the last to die is the muddled and selfish grandmother, who has inadvertently been responsible for getting them lost in the first place. Inarticulate with fear as she hears the rest of the family being shot one by one, she mutters, 'Jesus! Jesus!' and tries to tell the killer to pray.

' "Jesus was the only One that ever raised the dead," the Misfit continued, "and he shouldn't have done it. He thrown everything off balance. If He did what He said, then it's nothing for you to do but throw away everything and follow Him, and if He didn't, then it's

23. Flannery O'Connor, *The Complete Stories* (New York: Farrar, Strauss and Giroux, 1971) (henceforth CS).

nothing for you to do but enjoy the few minutes you got left the best way you can … It ain't right I wasn't there because if I had of been there I would of known and I wouldn't be like I am now." His voice seemed about to crack and the grandmother's head cleared for an instant. She saw the man's face twisted close to her own as if he were going to cry and she murmured, "Why you're one of my babies. You're one of my own children!" '[24]

He recoils and kills her. Why is this – as it is clearly intended to be[25] – a moment of 'grace'? Because, says O'Connor, 'she realizes, even in her limited way, that she is responsible for the man before her and joined to him by ties of kinship which have their roots deep in the mystery she has been merely prattling about so far'.[26] It is a risk-charged incident, veering towards sentimentality, then brutally pulled back. In Maritain's terms, it is an imaginative movement that takes hold of a 'pulsion', a connection or rhythm: something unites the grandmother and the criminal,

24. CS, p.132.
25. She discusses the story in MM, pp.109–13; cf. HB, pp.436–7.
26. MM, pp.111–12.

enables the grandmother to recognize some sense in which she is not only part of the same family as the Misfit but his parent, part of what has made him who he is. Her own petty sins and self-obsessions and self-delusions are involved in making a world in which he is possible; but her recognition of this is also a moment of compassion, not of self-loathing. So she speaks the truth, unusually, but in a way that is, as O'Connor suggests, not a denial of who we have found her to be in the whole narrative.

The same impulse is at work in O'Connor's second novel, *The Violent Bear it Away*, first published in 1955, though it is if anything even darker and more complex as an evocation of grace.[27] The work took her a long time to complete, and it is intriguing to see in one or two of the short stories of the early 1950s her first attempts at some of the themes and even characters

27. Published in the USA in 1960 by Farrar, Strauss and Giroux. I have referred to the London, Faber, 1980, edition with an introduction by Paul Bailey (the title alludes to Mt. 11.12, about the Kingdom of Heaven being subject to violence, 'and the violent bear it away' (from the – Roman Catholic – Douai translation of the Bible); henceforth VB.

of the finished work.[28] Briefly, this is a novel about obsession and rationality, and about faith and baptism. Mason Tarwater is a prophet, a vivid, grotesque old man living on a remote small-holding with his orphaned teenage great-nephew, Francis Marion Tarwater. He has abducted the boy from the home of his nephew, Francis's uncle, Rayber; just as, years before, he had taken Rayber himself from his indifferent and feckless parents. But Rayber had left him, rejecting the old man's faith and the prophetic vocation; he has married and has a mentally retarded son, now abandoned by his mother. The old man dies and Francis, with nowhere else to turn, hitches a ride to the city and lands up on Rayber's doorstep.

Old Tarwater has impressed on Francis that he must follow the prophetic calling too; and part of that vocation will be to baptize Rayber's little boy, Bishop. He will receive confirmatory signs as to when he must do this. Rayber greets the teenage boy with initial delight at the opportunity of educating him out of his blind and distorted faith. But young Tarwater is a profoundly

28. 'The River', CS, pp.157–74, is a story about baptism; 'You Can't Be Any Poorer Than Dead', CS, pp. 292–310, introduces some of the main characters of VB.

damaged, fearful, resentful child, who cannot shake off his great-uncle's presence; from the start, his relation with Bishop is charged with terror and panic, as Bishop stands for the calling he is eager to forget, yet cannot. As the story unfolds, we learn that Rayber, who loves the small child helplessly and mutely, has in the past tried to drown him, unable to bear the burden of his own compassion. He challenges and goads young Tarwater, increasingly despairing of making any contact; he admits to him his attempt to kill the child. Eventually Tarwater himself drowns the child – partly to prove to Rayber that he can do what Rayber can't, and to free himself from the haunting presence of the old man. As he kills the child, he finds himself saying the formula of baptism. He runs away in greater turmoil than ever, and is drugged and raped by a passing motorist. When he returns to the smallholding, he finds that his great-uncle's body – which he thought had been burned in the fire he kindled when he left the old house – has been properly buried by a black neighbour and the cross has been erected on the grave. All through the book, Tarwater has been unable to eat properly, fasting and vomiting; at this point he suddenly has a hallucinatory vision of the feeding of the five thousand (a scene described for him earlier by the old man as what lies ahead in heaven, provoking a sort of horror in the boy at a hunger that splits the bottom out of his stomach),[29] and he becomes 'aware at last of the object of his hunger, aware that it was the same as the old man's and that nothing on earth would fill him'. And he knows that he has no option but to 'sustain' that hunger, along with all those others throughout the ages, 'strangers from that violent country where the silence is never broken except to shout the truth'.[30]

Grace, but not as we know it? It is a story that shocked at the time of its publication and still has the capacity to make the reader intensely uneasy. Part of the unease is that the laconic narration unsettles any clarity about the emotional perspective we ought to be adopting. O'Connor's determination to keep the narrator invisible, speaking only through act and character, is rigorously sustained. The teenage boy's reported feelings are kept strictly within the frame of what is narratively possible for him –

29. VB, p.21.
30. VB, pp.241, 242.

an emotionally starved and injured child from one point of view; a fully grown sceptic and critic of what and who he encounters from another. We follow his perceptions but are given no easy handle for empathy. Paradoxically, the figure of Rayber, who represents what is in O'Connor's world most seriously destructive, is the one through whose eyes we see most, physically and emotionally; and because he is so manifestly the enemy of young Tarwater, we are left uncomfortable at the empathy he prompts. He utters the platitudes of a moderately educated progressive and sceptical pedagogue; but his inner life is as emotionally tormented as Tarwater's. His relatively greater self-awareness only serves to highlight the tension between his banal philosophy and his terrible internal suffering – the pain he feels in his love for both children, especially his love for Bishop, 'love without reason, love for something futureless, love that appeared to exist only for itself'.[31] And this 'horrifying love' will, he knows, overflow into the whole of his world if it is not kept focused on the child. He fails to kill him because he has 'a moment of complete terror in which he envisioned his life

31. VB, p.113.

without the child';[32] he cannot imagine living with that dreadful pointless compassion set free to seek for other objects. (The point is developed in a letter of July 1962 to Alfred Corn.[33])

So the revelation of grace, here as in 'A Good Man is Hard to Find', is a revelation of unseen solidarity. Young Tarwater is hungry for more than the world can supply; Rayber suffers resentfully and uncomprehendingly from the drag of a 'futureless' love that wants and needs only itself *as* love and seeks no outcome. They are both 'excessive' people, who are more than they are and see in the world more than it is. Yet they are both also appallingly wounded people. In a highly charged scene halfway through the book, Rayber discovers that Tarwater has left his house in the night to slip away to a church, where he hears a 6-year-old child preacher proclaiming the gospel. Rayber eavesdrops and hears the child speaking of the flight into Egypt: ' "The world hoped old Herod would slay the right child, the world hoped old Herod wouldn't waste those children, but he wasted them. He didn't get the

32. VB, p.142.
33. HB, p.484.

right one. Jesus grew up and raised the dead." '
And Rayber protests silently that Jesus did not
raise the dead the Lord himself had killed –
Tarwater, Bishop, himself as a child, children
scarred and ruined by their contact with him.[34]
By the end of the book, the question of dead
children has become central to the whole world
of the narrative. When Herod sets out to kill
Jesus, he kills every child but Jesus: Rayber and
Tarwater between them kill Bishop because both
are trying to kill Christ. But they are trying to
kill Christ because they have encountered grace
as a death sentence, so that their very lives have
come to depend apparently on the killing of the
possibility of grace.

This is no easy solidarity, not even the complex
recognition of the Misfit by the grandmother.
It is an uncovering of the tragic within grace;
the violence in love, to borrow Gillian Rose's
phrase.[35] Grace is concrete and specific, it raises
the dead; but, as the child evangelist goes on to
say, the world wants to say, 'Leave the dead lie.'
As with the Misfit – and as with Hazel Motes,

34. VB, p.132.
35. Gillian Rose, *The Broken Middle: Out of Our Ancient
Society* (Oxford: Blackwell, 1992), especially pp.148–52.

the central figure of O'Connor's first novel, *Wise Blood*, who founds the 'Church Without Christ'[36] – Jesus has 'thrown everything off balance'. And 'Rayber saw himself fleeing with the child to some enclosed garden where he would teach her the truth, where he would gather all the exploited children of the world and let the sunshine flood their minds.'[37] His passionate desire to teach children their mortality is both a real and disinterested love and a terrible longing to contain love within finite boundaries only. Teaching mortality alone is, it seems, itself fatal. No wonder that O'Connor said that she had spent most of the seven years of working on the novel refining the character of Rayber;[38] he could have been a caricature or a wholly unsympathetic figure – like the kindred character of Sheppard, the militant agnostic father in the later story, 'The Lame Shall Enter First', who, like Rayber, struggles to love an unlovable teenager into reasonable adult life and colludes in destroying his own small son in the process.[39] It reads almost as an alternative

36. *Wise Blood* (New York: Farrar, Strauss and Giroux, 1952).
37. VB, p.133.
38. HB, p.353.
39. CS, pp.445–82.

vehicle for issues not fully explored in the novel, the not-quite-finished business of the threefold relation of vulnerable child, rational father and adolescent disturber. She wrote in a letter about the kinship between Tarwater and the disturbed boy Johnson – 'one of his terrible cousins'[40] – in this story; and it is again a story of how passionate rationalism with its insistence on mortality combines with a distorted and obsessional relation with the divine to produce a real child's death. But she also admitted[41] that she had failed to get inside Sheppard. The early drafts of *The Violent Bear it Away* had obviously had the same problem, keeping Rayber at a distance emotionally; but much of the strength of the finished novel is in the extraordinary access we have to Rayber's inner world. It is utterly wrong to say, as did Paul Bailey in his introduction to the 1980 Faber edition of the novel, that she meant Rayber to be 'repugnant' and that her understanding of him was almost an accidental by-product of her art.[42] The truth is that his doomed and frustrated love is indispensable for

40. HB, p.456.
41. HB, p.491.
42. VB, p.viii.

the creation of the deepest tensions of the work, which have to do with his fearful awareness of his closeness to Tarwater.

O'Connor is insisting on a perception of grace that is *not* necessarily the introduction of a meaning or even an absolution (though there are powerful stories where absolution is precisely the crux, as in 'The Artificial Nigger'[43] and the late and splendid 'Revelation'[44]); grace is an excess that *may* make for significance or forgiveness, but needn't. Yet without the breakthrough to the level of hunger and 'futureless' passion, there is no forgiveness. O'Connor's impatience with readers and critics who complained about the anti-humanistic distortion of her vision or the cruelty of her picture of God is understandable. A 'humanism' that denied the facts of mental and

43. CS, pp.249–70. The title is deeply distasteful to the modern reader; O'Connor 'uses the prevailing locution of the South as easily, and as unmaliciously, as it often occurs there, among blacks and whites alike', says the editor of HB, rather too blandly (p.xvii). But this editor does admit that O'Connor's attitudes to race are in many respects a blind spot. See Woods, *op. cit.*, Chapter 3, for a fuller discussion.
44. CS, pp.488–509.

physical suffering and above all of the capacity of the human mind for untruth would be ultimately murderous; her narrative is out to show how literally true that is. A God who fails to generate desperate hunger and confused and uncompromising passion is no God at all. It is not that Tarwater's life and faith are held up as a model of or for anything; they are what they are. And they are what they are because God is as God is, not an agent within the universe, not a source of specialized religious consolation. If God is real, the person in touch with God is in danger, at any number of levels. And to awaken the hunger that Tarwater at last recognizes is to risk creating in people a longing too painful to bear or a longing that will lead them to take such risks that it seems indeed nakedly cruel to expose them to that hunger in the first place.

This Dostoevskian grimness is at the heart of 'The Lame Shall Enter First', in which Johnson, the teenage petty criminal, refuses the 'salvation' offered by Sheppard because 'Nobody can save me but Jesus.'[45] He knows he is morally and spiritually corrupt in a way that only repentance

45. CS, p.478.

can heal; he knows he risks hell. And very deliberately he sets out to introduce Sheppard's own child, Norton, to this world of impossible hope – to 'corrupt' him in Sheppard's eyes. Norton longs to know if his dead mother still exists; Sheppard gives an uncompromising no, Johnson an equally uncompromising yes. But where she is, 'you got to be dead to get there'. Eventually Norton, desperate for a love his father cannot show and ecstatically confident that he can go to meet his mother, hangs himself. So too, in the earlier story, 'The River', an unloved child ends up embracing death: taken out for the day by a local woman to a revival meeting, he is baptized by another of O'Connor's alarming child evangelists (a teenager this time), who tells him that 'You count now … You didn't even count before.'[46] But what has changed for him? Life with his parents is the same, lived against the background of their dim Bohemianism and cynicism, and he is thirsty for the river of life to which the young preacher has opened his eyes. He heads back to the river, determined to baptize himself once again. 'For an instant he was overcome with surprise: then, since he was moving quickly and

46. CS, p.168.

knew that he was getting somewhere, all his fear and fury left him.'[47]

Death as 'getting somewhere' is a typically brutal piece of O'Connor irony. You can see why critics mutter about a denial of life in her fiction; but her point is, as she almost despaired of making clear, that the juxtaposing of God and these terrible moments of fatal longing is the only possible hopeful perspective on such moments. When hunger is faced without illusion, in the way she argues only a believer can face it, what the artist achieves is exactly the representation of what Maritain calls the 'woundedness' of the world in its entirety. Without the evocation (not invocation) of God in these narratives, the scope of the human actuality would be denied or reduced. Sheppard and Rayber would be right in seeing the awfulness of the prophetic calling and what another lateish story, 'The Enduring Chill', calls 'purifying terror', as essentially a disease to be extirpated from the human self. With another twist of irony, 'The Everlasting Chill' charts the progress of a pretentious and selfish young man who believes he is romantically dying

47. CS, p.174.

of some appropriately dramatic disease towards the recognition that he will live, an invalid with a chronic medical problem that is inexorably unromantic; as he comes to terms with this, he feels the first stirrings of actual faith. He has been dispossessed of his death and given life – life, like everyone else's, lived under the shadow of ordinary, boring mortality. And his dispossession opens him to a truth both utterly undramatic and terrifying, 'a chill so peculiar, so light, that it was like a warm ripple across a deeper sea of cold'.[48] His previous hectic rationalism has been a denial that looked logically to a death which would seal once and for all his rightness and his uniqueness. Illness refuses him death and gives him mortality; it refuses to let him ignore the time he will have to live, refuses his own denial. The irony is that the gift of life is the gift of daily 'terror', the terror of being aware of reality in the light of God.

48. CS, p.382.

3

What O'Connor has to say about the particular reasons why the Catholic novelist has the liberty to leave nothing out of his view becomes more and more clear as we look at her actual practice as a writer. The convergence between the real and the good which is axiomatic for her, as for Jones and Maritain, is far from being the acceptance of a world in which human choices and human contingency produce terrible outcomes, terrible in their tragedy and their comedy alike. Nor is she saying that any situation is 'redeemable' (that would be dangerously close to the illusions of a Rayber). It is primarily just that every human desire or disposition *signifies*, and so is worth narrating, worth transubstantiating into the words of narrative. Explanation is reduction; it is trying to contain another in your own identity. Old Tarwater reads an article about him by Rayber and is incensed at the plot to capture him 'inside his head';[49] young Tarwater echoes this in his protest to Rayber when the latter tries to find out the extent of his literacy: 'I'm free … I'm outside your head.'[50] So

49. VB, p.20.
50. VB, p.111.

the narrator steps back from seeking to effect and control a specific emotional reaction to a character; as we have seen, O'Connor deliberately confuses our sympathies in ways that not every critic seems to recognize. We see through young Tarwater's eyes, but what we see is overwhelmingly unclear and shot through with his rebellion as well as his obsessive religious haunting. We see through Rayber's eyes, but what we see is also his impotence before the absolute otherness of both the children whom he longs to embrace and make sense of. We are not given a stable judgement in the way the story is told; and when Tarwater finally accepts his vocation, we are left with the sense of the rightness or intelligibility of this in terms of all that has happened to him – not least his encounter with another level of embodied evil in the rapist – but not with a justification that can be hooked on to anything outside the drama of the persons created in the telling. The necessity of Tarwater's calling has to emerge from the necessity that the world of the fiction has created. The reader is free to believe Tarwater and his great-uncle equally deluded. The reader cannot be 'inside' the author's head, because the freedom of the characters within the story has to be evoked in the reader.

But what the narrative will have done is to oblige the reader to see what it is to inhabit their universe and not to run to the explanations that Rayber has to offer, explanations which license us not really to attend to the world of the Tarwaters as an inhabitable world, a significant world. Rayber and the Tarwaters are alike 'outside' an authorial head to the extent that they embody 'necessities' that arise from something other than the artist's individual will.

The cultivation of the will in order to shape your own identity is what is involved in the moral life, and the narrator – O'Connor agrees with Maritain – doesn't need moral rectitude *as* narrator: 'rectitude of the appetite' is incidental to all art.[51] Freedom is at work in both art and prudence, as David Jones reminds us, but there is a difference between the choices that a person makes for the good of their soul and the choices made for the good of the work. 'The Catholic novelist doesn't have to be a saint; he doesn't even have to be a Catholic; he does, unfortunately, have to be a novelist.'[52] And the primary task then becomes

51. HB, pp.123–4, MM, pp.171–2.
52. MM, p.172.

'the accurate naming of the things of God'.[53] It is striking that Francis Tarwater, at the beginning of the story, is frightened by the old man's insistence on his calling because 'It was as if he were afraid that if he let his eye for an instant longer than was needed to place something – a spade, a hoe, the mule's hind quarters before his plow, the red furrow under him – that the thing would suddenly stand before him, strange and terrifying, demanding that he name it and name it justly and be judged for the name he gave it. He did all he could to avoid this threatened intimacy of creation.'[54] We may remember Jones's account of the artist's 'intimacy' with the world as one of the poles of human engagement with the environment. What O'Connor seems to be saying is that the attention given to this intimate summons to name (and so to change) what is there in front of you is a suspension of artistic control so as to let the inner necessities of the subject – in this case, the imagined person – unfold. And it is the opposite of the immediate 'placing' of the thing or person seen that is the habitual mode of human operation. As Tarwater's own

53. HB, p.128.
54. VB, pp.21–2.

movement is traced, we can see that his final baptizing of Bishop is a response to just this demand for a *naming*; at last, he and he alone can give the child a name that says who he most seriously is, God's child. The process of learning that name is agonizing and protracted, inseparably bound up with the destructiveness that is generated by the conflicting pressures of the two worlds Tarwater has to cope with. But at last he himself becomes an 'artist' in becoming a prophet; as O'Connor says, the vision of the artist of fiction is prophetic vision, that 'realism of distance' we have already noted.[55] The ethic of the artist, if we can speak in such terms, is detachment, dispossession of the desire to hold everything inside your own head.

I have devoted a fair amount of attention to O'Connor's second novel because it so densely and subtly brings together the themes of her whole aesthetic. She takes baptism for her theme, not in order to perform a simple apologetic job of persuading the reader that baptism is a Good Thing, but to establish that it is a *serious* affair and one that is crucial in grounding and

55. MM, p.170.

contextualizing an entire system of perceiving, of doing maximal justice to the visible world. To arrive at the point where the world can be truthfully named in its relation to God involves some grasp of the world as object of pointless, 'futureless' love; it must therefore involve levels of bewilderment, deep emotional confusion and frustration in the process, even a blurring of the boundaries between love and rejection (since we are understandably frightened of replacing ordinary human affection with this radical and disabling love). And the recognition that the world can never be loved enough is bound in with the recognition of the 'hunger' at the heart of human identity: if ordinary food is consistently rejected as not enough, what is it that sustains that hunger? It may be a depth of emotional and psychological bondage and injury that has terminally disabled a person's appetite. It may indeed be the kind of sickness that Rayber so deeply believes it to be. But what if this diagnosis so shrinks the actuality of the hungry believer that it also becomes a deeply dangerous, even terminal disabling of any relation with them? The narrator has to make this last question as pressing as possible if the credibility of this particular sort of 'naming' of the world represented by baptism is to be vindicated or at least established as serious. And part of the pressing of that question is also a tracing of unseen or unacknowledged solidarities between agents who are on utterly different paths. As O'Connor laconically puts it in 1962, 'Tarwater wrestles with the Lord and Rayber wins';[56] both are exploring their freedom before God, and only fully make narrative sense in that relation with each other.

O'Connor is largely a faithful theoretical follower of Maritain; but she, like Jones, takes him further than perhaps he would easily want to go. Certainly she might come under Maritain's strictures about deliberately setting out to shock; though I think she would respond by saying that the artist has an obligation to find the tone or register in which she can actually be heard, and an artist presenting a Christian universe cannot but shock. This must be defensible so long as it is actually a strategy for the truth, not a flexing of the artistic muscles for its own sake. I suspect that this is one of those areas where she found Maritain 'soft'; and perhaps the pervasiveness of the musical analogy in Maritain was equally a problem.

56. HB, p.488.

O'Connor does not seem to be responding to the sense of a buried rhythm or consonance exactly. And yet, her irony depends on something like this; people are bound together in both the seeking for God and the rejection of God and their acknowledgement of the reality of being together in rejection can trigger a sense of the other solidarity – as in the conclusion of 'The Displaced Person', one of her bleakest tales, where the momentary and frightening revelation of collusion in hatred brings about a crisis that might lead (though we don't know within the narrative) to a moment of grace.[57] Here her chief character is marked throughout by an unreasoning prejudice against the devout, hardworking refugee who arrives on the farm and is hated by the other employees – to the point where she and they allow the refugee to be crushed to death in an accident that they could have prevented. The recognition of solidarity in hatred produces the dramatic crisis of a physical and psychological collapse; the story ends with the wry and patient Catholic priest visiting Mrs Mcintyre, waiting for her to see the further connection that alone can set her free – death or faith or both.

57. CS, pp.194–235.

We are some way from the language of 'pulsions'; but the whole point of narrative irony is a disruption of the politics of appearances to redraw the map of relations between the agents in the narrative. It is, as was suggested earlier, the handling of irony that is most distinctive to O'Connor; it acknowledges that the artist's challenge to appearances is necessarily a challenge to how we appear to ourselves, that the stories we tell about ourselves are pervaded by motivations, connections, interests that we either deny or know nothing of. The narrator too tells a story whose full pattern of interconnections he or she cannot know, so that an ironic storyteller must stand back, must strive for dispossession in respect of the story being told and its agents, fully aware that final dispossession is not possible. Hence, for the Christian narrator above all, the act of telling a story about human agents who do not know themselves while vulnerable to the same deceits as those characters is itself potentially both a comic and a tragic matter, in which a measure of absurdity attends both characters and narrator. Once more we find ourselves in territory not charted by Maritain – but as the result of a meeting between his theory and a specific artistic practice.

Comedy, O'Connor argues, depends on theological conviction.[58] If nothing is unjustifiable, nothing is absurd. Perhaps we should expand the dictum of Dostoevsky, that underrated comic genius: 'If God does not exist, everything is permitted', he said; but for O'Connor, if God does not exist, nothing is ridiculous. The examination of Flannery O'Connor's fiction leaves us with a clear sense of the artist's task as involving a recognition of the inherently ludicrous element in art, the constant doomed effort to let go of objects, characters, that the artist has created. But the more this recognition is achieved, the more the connections can appear that do not belong simply in an artist's will and decision, the more the work can embody both the freedom and the necessity of the actual finite world and the material produced by the artist can communicate the excess of reality. O'Connor was in a number of senses an artist of excess; but not the least of her gifts was to suggest that the perception of excess can generate perspectives that are equally and painfully appalling and comical. You might even say that this was how she made concrete in her storytelling the strangeness of an unconditional love.

58. MM, pp.167–8.

So we shall move on to some reflection on the artist and the love of God, the question of whether art is finally possible without the sacred. If O'Connor is right, the least we could say would be that belief in the Christian dogma both offers and enjoins a radically unselective range of material for the artist. As she wrote, 'When people have told me that because I am a Catholic, I cannot be an artist, I have had to reply, ruefully, that because I am a Catholic, I cannot afford to be less than an artist.'[59]

59. MM, p.146.

FOUR

God and
the Artist

What is the world that art takes for granted? It is one in which perception is always incomplete. Instead of a scheme where stimulus is followed by determinate response, there is constantly more response evoked; and the fact of response itself becomes a datum for the mind. Telling the truth about what is before us is not a matter of exhaustively defining the effects of certain phenomena on the receptors of brain and sense. In a celebrated book, Douglas R. Hofstadter plays a set of brilliant variations on the theme of what is happening at different levels when a single group of phenomena stimulates the brain: alternative descriptions are both possible and imperative; and the feedback from one set of perceptions becomes inseparably linked with what is subsequently 'seen' in the initial phenomena.[1] Consciousness, to use one of Hofstadter's key metaphors, is *fugal*: the following of one set of clues or triggers sets off another

1.   Douglas R. Hofstadter and Daniel C. Dennett (eds), *The Mind's Eye. Fantasies and Reflections on Self and Soul* (London: Penguin Books, 1981). Hofstadter's dialogues on the nature of consciousness (chaotically witty and almost unmanageably wide-ranging) appear on pp.69–95, 149–201 and 430–60. It is the second of these to which I shall be making reference.

trajectory, *generates* another series of moves. And Hofstadter's conclusion is that we cannot finally talk about the mind or the brain as a self-contained system for receiving external stimuli. On the one hand, we cannot produce a physical map that will show us 'where or how beliefs are coded' in the brain;[2] on the other, there is no immaterial subject, no ghost in the machine, whose identity is given prior to the history of involvement with stimuli. 'Mind is a pattern perceived by a mind' is Hofstadter's suggested formula: 'the self-awareness comes from the system's intricately intertwined responses to both internal and external stimuli'.[3] And this presupposes a difference between a *signal* – which triggers a reaction but has no meaning in itself – and a *symbol*, which is already a complex bundle of interrelated elements, a meaningful reality. A symbol is intrinsically bound up with the *relation* of things sensed and lodged in the subject, it is part of a system of seeing or absorbing what is there; and so it necessarily generates further symbolic connections, not merely a repeatable, generalizable response.[4] Mental activity instantly

2. Ibid., p.200.
3. Ibid.
4. Ibid., pp.176–8.

combines – complicates – signals into symbols; recognition is never simply of an isolated stimulus – or perhaps we should say that recognition at such a level is so deeply buried in the process of the mind that it cannot even be intelligibly described.

So that part of the material world that is the human system of knowing cannot be spoken of except as a spiral of self-extending symbolic activity; its relation to its environment is inescapably mobile, time-related. There is no way of abstracting from the passage of time some necessary, non-revisable and exhaustive correlation between an inside and an outside, a set of determinate, entirely 'objective' stimuli and a 'correct' reception of and reaction to them. This is in no way to say that there is no truthful relation between speech and reality, or however you want to put it. The process is one of generation, not creation from nothing, and what can be said is not decided by an inner 'free' subject involved in endless self-reflection. What you can meaningfully say is constrained by what is given. But truthfulness unfolds – it doesn't happen all at once – and makes possible different levels of appropriating or sharing in the activity that is the world. Basic

to all this is – though it is not quite the conclusion that Hofstadter himself would want to arrive
at – a sense of the real as active rather than static,
a mobile pattern whose best analogy is indeed
musical, not mechanical. This dimension of active
life *here* makes possible this dimension *here*; what
is enacted and seen in one place is 'lived again' in
another, so that what is involved in knowing something is more like re-enacting a performance
than labelling an object. Knowing re-presents;
which means that whatever stimulus starts the
process off is not adequately thought of as a
fixed entity requiring no more than a single
identification.

The relation between knower and known envis-
aged here is remarkably similar to the 'participation' spoken of in the more traditional idiom of
scholastic and Platonic thinking. There is some
activity which, beginning in the object known,
continues to exercise a characteristic mode of life
in another medium: the material in which it is
first embodied does not exhaust the formal life
that is at work. The 'what' of what is known is
not something that simply belongs to the given
shape we begin with in our perception; it extends
possibilities, or even, to use a question-begging

word, *invites* response that will continue and re-form its life, its specific energy. All this is implied in Maritain's words, which have resonated so frequently in our discussions, 'things are not only what they are'. Re-presentation assumes that there is excess in what presents itself for knowing, and that neither the initial cluster of perceptions nor any one set of responses will finally succeed in containing what is known. Thus what I perceive or know is always oriented to more than my perception; it is at least potentially related to something that is identical neither with the 'given' shape or structure, nor with the structure as my mind initially conceives and constructs it. The claim that this or that conceptual form is identical with the living form of what is encountered would deny this excess of potential outside the present relation with me as knower, and so would assert implicitly that the object's being 'for me' at this moment of perception is all there is to it. But this does not mean, as some philosophical traditions have wanted to say, that there is a fixed 'for itself' hidden in what is perceived, standing over against the 'for me' dimension. As we have been arguing, the inner life of a reality is what unfolds in time, generating more and more symbolic structures, not a timeless and relation-free definition.[5] That the structure of what is experienced and thought is involved with the symbolic structure of mind in the way Hofstadter proposes means that the life of the object in the knowing mind is genuinely in some sense an aspect of the object's own life – not a construct by an independent thinking substance working on dead or static material presented to it as a determined set of data.

These philosophical issues are closely bound up with what we have been looking at in this series of lectures. Art, as has been suggested to us at many points of our enquiry, is unintelligible if it is not what we might call an acute case of knowledge in general. It is that form of intellectual life in which the generativity of

5. On interiority as connected with the taking and the passing of time, cf. Gillian Rose, *Mourning Becomes the Law. Philosophy and Representation* (Cambridge University Press, 1996), Chapters 5 and 6; also Rowan Williams, 'The suspicion of suspicion: Wittgenstein and Bonhoeffer', in Richard H. Bell (ed.), *The Grammar of the Heart. New Essays in Moral Philosophy and Theology* (San Francisco: Harper and Row, 1988).

140

the world we encounter and experience is allowed to work in ways that are free from many of the requirements of routine instrumental thinking (remember the distinction mentioned in the first of these lectures between symmetric and asymmetric thought). When we are tempted to confine our vision of mental activity to the successful manipulation of defined objects and the solving of practical problems as to how we negotiate with such objects, we need to recognize that this is not all. We still have to 'negotiate' with stimuli or data which do not lend themselves to treatment of this kind – with the chain of interaction set up by what we encounter, in the history of other encounters, in our own history as subjects, in the allusions and cross-references set up. There is an insanity in which hidden connections are everything, in which the excess of symbolism becomes the habitual climate of thought; but there is equally an insanity in which excess is denied and the world reduced to that series of problems which my mind currently happens to engage. From the point of view of this latter insanity, the realm of excess, of symbolic generativity, is at best an idle form of play decided upon by the individual will, or else a plain pathology.[6] Meaning here would relate only to the system of solving problems that I now employ; I should be allowing no sense of the meaning that is not 'for me', that exists in relation to something other than me.

Hence the claim that art has an 'ontology' implicit in it. It is not decorative or arbitrary but grounded in what we ought to call a kind of obedience. The artist struggles to let the logic of what is there display itself in the particular concrete matter being worked with. The teasing language of the fiction writer claiming not to know what his or her characters are going to do illustrates this most plainly, perhaps. 'I doubt myself if many writers know what they are going to do when they start out', wrote Flannery O'Connor;

6. See the essay of Michael Maltby quoted above in Chapter 1. For another psychoanalytic diagnosis of the risks of an exclusively functional approach to creativity, see Michael Parsons, *The Dove that Returns, the Dove that Vanishes. Paradox and Creativity in Psychoanalysis* (London: Routledge, 2000), especially Chapters 3 and 9. Parsons notes (p.170) that his view of creativity 'does not see that process as being secondary to anything, nor as any kind of corrective or compensatory activity, but as a central expression of what it means to be human'.

'When I started writing that story ['Good Country People'], I didn't know there was going to be a PhD with a wooden leg in it.'[7] The example is specially salient, since it is clear that, in this story, the one-leggedness of the woman in question is a metaphor for another kind of disability or imbalance. O'Connor is claiming that instead of beginning from some kind of search for a metaphor, the imagination shapes a character whose own structural integrity within the fiction produces an excess of meaning which offers a metaphorical possibility. In any serious fiction, it is worth asking whether character or metaphor comes first in this sort of context: fiction may symbolize, but it must do so by way of both over- and under-determination. A character may have fluid and plural symbolic generativity; or a character may have no clear line of symbolic resonance beyond what any agent in a narrative has. What matters is the inner coherence of the person drawn. Absent this, we have once again the artist's will emerging as the motor force in composition; no obedience, no sense of an imperative.

It is worth digressing very briefly to note how Dostoevsky's drafts for his fiction demonstrate

7.   O'Connor, MM, p.100.

this in depth. As is well known, the characters and plot of *The Idiot* in particular went through a strikingly large number of major recastings, chronicled in Dostoevsky's notebooks.[8] David Magarshack, introducing the Penguin edition of the novel, comments that, 'The idea that the characters take such a hold of the author that they write themselves obviously does not apply to Dostoevsky.'[9] But this surely misses the point: Dostoevsky is, you could say, struggling to find characters that he can 'obey', that do indeed take hold and that he can therefore trace with coherence and integrity. He began the novel's drafts

---

8. David Magarshack, introducing his 1955 Penguin translation of *The Idiot*, summarizes the immensely complex history of Dostoevsky's planning for this novel. There is also some seminal discussion in George Steiner, *Tolstoy or Dostoevsky*, 2nd edn (London: Penguin Books, 1967), pp. 140–67.

9. Magarshack's introduction to *The Idiot*, p.23. Contrast Steiner, *op. cit.*, p.167: 'The German dramatist Hebbel asked how far any personage invented by a poet could be thought "objective". He gave his own reply: "So far as man is free in his relations to God." The degree of Muishkin's objectivity, the extent to which he resisted Dostoevsky's total control, can be documented in the drafts … A dramatist can know only "so much" about his personages.'

with the idea of someone who advances to some sort of holiness through a career of extreme moral behaviour; it is the 'innocence' of his violent extremism that carries him through to renewal. But the various plans failed to work themselves out. Gradually the central figure – epileptic, vulnerable, capable of drastic and shocking acts of forgiveness – came into focus as a representation, from his first appearance, of Christian love, and Dostoevsky clearly thought at one stage that he was constructing a 'Christ figure'[10] A good many commentators have taken him at his word; but this, too, misses the point. The final version of this enigmatic character is in one sense an embodiment of Christian gentleness, but it is a gentleness deeply flawed by lack of self-knowledge, confused desire and passivity – an ironic picture that reflects what some would indeed see as Christlikeness, yet incorporates an oblique recognition of something like a Nietzschean critique of Christianity as dealing in unrealities and depending on the resentment of the weak. Myshkin as he emerges in the novel is a tragic hero in a sense that prevents him being a simple icon of Christ (though Dostoevsky mischievously gives him the physiognomy

10. Magarshack, p.21.

of the familiar iconography of the Saviour, and has people wondering where they have seen him before).[11] The important issue is that Dostoevsky failed to write either a novel about the conversion of a sinner or the portrait of a saint; he wrote one of his most painfully enigmatic fictions because he could not 'find' the character of either saint or sinner, and so produced a singular, complex character whose depth is precisely in his failure to be either saint or sinner, his sheer marginality in what we ordinarily think of as the moral world. He is a 'Christ figure' in his alienness to mere morality; but – human and not divine – this alienness destroys him and implicates him in the destruction of others. The haunting reminiscence of Christ that Myshkin carries with him is a matter of intensely ironic imagining, not a pious aura. Here as elsewhere, Bakhtin is a necessary voice to remind us of Dostoevsky's refusal to write in straight lines.[12]

11. On Myshkin's appearance, see *The Idiot*, p.28; cf. Steiner, *op.cit.*, p.150.
12. Steiner, *op.cit.*, pp.141, 265–6, 296 on the ambiguity of Myshkin's status as a 'Christ figure'. Mikhail Bakhtin, *Problems of Dostoevsky's Poetics* (Ann Arbor: Ardis, 1973) is his main text on Dostoevsky's dialogic technique. It is worth comparing the shadows around the role of Myshkin in *The Idiot* with the complex central character, the deaf-mute, in Carson McCullers, *The Heart is a Lonely Hunter*.

The struggle chronicled in Dostoevsky's note-books is like David Jones's agonies over his later visual and poetic work; the connections are felt but the visible form eludes, and it is no use pre-tending, issuing a premature report on the work in hand or claiming it is finished when it isn't. You have to find what you must obey, artistically; and finding it is finding that which exists in rela-tion to more than your will and purpose – finding the depth of alternative embodiment in the seen landscape, the depth of gratuitous capa-city in the imagined character (when what you *want* to imagine will not come) and so on. Ima-gination produces not a self-contained mental construct but a vision that escapes control, that brings with it its shadow and its margins, its absences and ellipses, a *dimensional* existence as we might call it. The degree to which art is 'obedient' – not dependent on an artist's deci-sions or tastes – is manifest in the degree to which the product has dimension outside of its relation to the producer, the sense of alternative space around the image, of real time and contingency in narrative, of hinterland. As we noted with Flannery O'Connor, the artist looks for the 'necessity' in the thing being made, but this 'necessity' can only be shown when the actual

147

artistic form somehow lets you know that the necessity is not imposed by the hand of an artistic will but uncovered as underlying the real contingency of a world that has been truthfully imagined, with its own proper time and space, its own causality and coherence.

2

To speak of art as having 'dimension' in this way is to say that the artist is always concerned with things as they are in relation to something more and other than the artist.[13] This holds true at both ends, so to speak, of the process of artistic labour. The artist perceives the material of the world – visible things, patterns of sound, texture – as offering more than can appear in one moment of encounter and so begins to produce a further thing in the world that will allow that unseen or unheard life to continue itself in another mode. But that further thing itself has to be set free from the artist's mental world to relate to unimagined observers or listeners in present and future. The artist does not exhaust the significance of his or her labour, but creates an object, a schema of perceptible data, that will have about it the same excess as the phenomena that stimulated the production in the first place. Art moves from and into a depth in the perceptible world that is contained

13. See Rowan Williams, 'Has secularism failed? Notes on the survival of the spirit' (2002 Raymond Williams Memorial Lecture at the Hay Festival of Literature), *Scintilla 7*, pp. 9–20.

neither in routine perception nor in the artist's conscious or unconscious purposes. George Steiner's appeal to 'real presence' in art is an important corrective to the mythology of art as wilful play;[14] but we could go further. The 'presence' in art is not some looming romantic/creative genius in the background, but a presence *within* what is made that generates difference, self-questioning, in the perceiving subject. It makes us present to ourselves in a fresh way, and so engages us in dialogue with ourselves as well as with the object and with the artist and with what the artist is responding to.

This suggests – nothing novel here – that bad art is art that does not invite us to question our perceptions or emotions, that imposes an intrusive artistic presence, that obscures both the original occasion of encounter, the original object in the world, and its own concrete life (by drawing attention to its message or willed meaning). The artist doing his job withdraws in the process of making so that this complex interaction of presences can occur. And this involves a dual act

14. George Steiner, *Real Presences. Is There Anything in What We Say?* (London: Faber, 1989).

of respect or reverence towards the world that is first seen or heard and towards the object. Remember Maritain's principle that the artist 'must be in love with what he is doing';[15] and being in love is normally thought to mean delighting in the simple actuality of the other. It is not a matter of sentimental feeling about the creations of an artist's imagination; it is a serious and costly dispossession of the artist in the work. And this in turn is not primarily about the virtues of impersonality in artistic technique, a plea for the classical over the romantic. The romantic too has to deal with what love for what is made demands, with the requirement of letting the work develop in its own logic, its own space. Classical art has its own temptations and sins; as Maritain hints, it may obscure the originating sense of congruence or confluence, the 'pulsion' that stimulates formal composition, by over-insistence on an abstract rigour of structure.[16]

Observing the integrity of what is made is the mode of the artist's love, a love that may be devoted as much to a monstrous creation as to a

15. *Art and Scholasticism*, p.48.
16. Above, pp.27ff.

superficially lovable one. Flannery O'Connor loves Rayber as a creation; we know this because she allows him his own poignant and surprising voice, and it has nothing to do with whether she likes or approves of him. Goya, we could say, 'loves' his depictions of the brutalities of the Peninsular War, not because he relishes cruelty in itself but because he paints what is there, not what he wants to see, and is acutely aware of the risk of representing such horrors.[17] If we ask where the boundary lies between this sort of love and a potentially corrupting involvement in the ugliness or cruelty of what is represented, the answer would perhaps have to be the degree of connection with the artist's individual emotional agenda. It is not always easy to identify pornography in art, but – whether we are thinking of cruelty in general or sexual violence in particular – one criterion is surely that the artist's emotional satisfaction becomes distractingly visible in the work. When this happens, there is a 'presence' in the work that disrupts the

17. See Susan Sontag, *Regarding the Pain of Others* (London: Hamish Hamilton, 2003), pp.39–42 on Goya's *Los Desastros de la Guerra*: 'While the image, like every image, is an invitation to look, the caption, more often than not, insists on the difficulty of doing just that' (p.40).

encounter of the reality represented and the person contemplating the work. It does not vitiate the beauty or the resourcefulness of the work; it is present in the work of a good many really significant artists, and is indeed part of the complex tissue of most imaginative labour; it is what makes the viewer uneasy with Caravaggio or Dali at times, or perhaps with some of Tennyson or Hughes.

But the artist's dispossession stands in a rather tangled relation to what she is working on and with. She is responding to some formal life or activity sensed and answered in the appearances she encounters; and it is a formal life or activity constantly on the edge of abandoning its phenomenal shape so as to be reshaped in another medium. The artist may be a 'hunter of forms', but the life that the artist engages with is a shedder of forms, dispossessing itself of this or that shape so as to be understood and remade. We return yet again to Maritain's dictum about things being more than they are. And there are several directions in which we might travel from this point. There is the implication that the world is not yet as it 'really' is; that the act of understanding and representation is bound up with the actual life of the material order. There is the possible hidden assumption in that idea that the world's reality is always asymptotically approaching its fullness by means of the response of imagination – the assumption of an 'ideal' fullness of perception in which things reach their destiny. There is the sense that the world 'gives' itself to be understood in the very moment when we realize that describing it simply in terms of how it relates to me, let alone serves my interest, is an inadequate or actively untruthful perspective. And all these trajectories lead towards the frontiers of theology. If there is *always*, that to which things are related irrespective of what I can (literally and metaphorically) make of them, that awareness of a depth in the observable world beyond what is at any moment observable is close to what seems to be meant by 'the sacred'. The appropriate response to the environment is necessarily something beyond the functional, a recognition of what is there in its own right or for its own sake. The human mind's distinctiveness seems to lie in its responsibility for drawing out what is not yet seen or heard in the material environment – but not solely in exploiting it for use but in facilitating its constant movement from one material form to another, its generative capacity. As David Jones would have delighted to point out, the product of art is as old as the tool in terms of what can be identified as specifically human. And the dynamic of generative capacity in what is encountered suggests what Hans Urs von Balthasar calls 'the freedom of the object', the element of gratuitous energy in the world's life that again corresponds to what we can call the sacred.[18]

Or rather, of course, what we call God. 'The sacred' is commonly a category of our perception, almost an aesthetic category; it does not capture that sense of energy, action or initiative that arises around the questions we have just been considering.[19] Balthasar speaks of how every finite phenomenon 'reveals the non-necessity of creaturely

18. It is a theme developed by Balthasar early in his *Theologik I. Wahrheit der Welt* (Einsiedeln: Johannes Verlag, 1985). For an excellent summary, see Aidan Nichols, *Say It Is Pentecost. A Guide Through Balthasar's Logic* (Edinburgh: T. and T. Clark, 2001), pp.23–7.
19. Ben Rogers (ed.), *Is Nothing Sacred?* (London: Routledge, 2004) is a collection of essays by agnostic humanists attempting to salvage some meaning for the term 'sacred'; their efforts illustrate eloquently the difficulty of using the word in a way unrelated to the reality of some different level of being.

existence and thus the Creator's *freedom*.[20] Something in the world of phenomena exceeds what is 'needed'; there is no final account of how things are that confines itself to function. One of the greatest misunderstandings of popular modernity is the notion that when we have, like good Darwinians, identified the function of various developments in various life-forms, we have thereby demonstrated their necessity; when the truth is that we have not begun to answer the question, 'Why precisely this?' or 'Was this the only possible resolution to an evolutionary conundrum?' The artist's commitment to generative excess in the world stands as a challenge to a vulgarized Darwinism: this life could be otherwise; this life could mean more than its adaptation to these particular circumstances suggests. The world 'makes itself other', not simply by endless environmental adjustment but by provoking the exploration and 're-formation' of which art is one cardinal element. But when we have said this, have we opened the door to that which is – to paraphrase a great Platonic phrase – 'in excess of being'?[21]

20. Balthasar, *Theologik I*, p.106.
21. The Good is *epekeina tēs ousias*, 'beyond being', according to the *Republic* 509B.

This could surely, though, be no more than the sense of inexhaustible depth within the environment we inhabit; do we need to say more, to suppose an ultimate otherness behind the reality we ordinarily acknowledge? The artist may well describe his work in relation to the sacred as I have been implicitly defining it without sensing the need to move from there to 'God'. And to this, the only answer the believer can properly give is to appeal to the constant pattern of 'making other' that runs through the reality the artist encounters. At each point, the process can be seen in terms of one aspect or level of the world re-forming, re-embodying itself in something radically different. To suppose that at the heart of this or at the end of the tracing of it to its first principles lies an ultimate sameness, simply an endless interiority within the world, ought to strike us as in some way jarring. The theologian will say that at that heart or that end is an irreducible difference – or rather two closely related differences – upon which all 'making other' depends. What these differences are needs further elucidation.

3

It would be foolish to claim that the practice of art constitutes some kind of argument for God's existence, and that is not my aim here. But it may well be that the practice of art assists us in making sense of what theologians, Christians in particular, claim to be the fundamental framework for 'reading' the world. Briefly, the Christian theologian says that God is, of his nature, 'generative' – that the notion of a solitary or inactive deity is incompatible with what God shows of God in the world and its history.[22] The doctrine of the trinity is not a conceptual tour de force to resolve a set of abstract puzzles. It is a statement that the God encountered in the history of Israel and the life of Christ must of necessity be involved in the generating of otherness because of the radical, self-dispossessing character of the love that this God displays. Yet this cannot mean that the world is necessary to God, that it exists to solve God's problems or serve God's needs; that would be to reduce the world to a level of unfreedom. Its being itself would have

22. The argument goes back to Athanasius in the fourth century, and is central to von Balthasar's theology; see Nichols, *op. cit.*, Chapters 13 and 14.

to be what God was specifying with the goal of meeting his supposed divine needs; gratuity would be an illusion. Hence the delicate balance of classical Christian metaphysics: God in the intrinsic 'necessity' of the divine life itself (constrained by nothing but the character of divine love and liberty) generates the eternal other, the partner of divine action, the Word or Son, and also the bearer of the inexhaustibility of divine life who is defined neither as Father nor as Son but simply as Spirit (so that divine life is not enclosed in a simple relation of logical opposition or symmetry).

And because of this timeless 'making other' that is intrinsic to God's being, the characteristic activity of God continues to be 'making other': the world comes into being by God's free decision, both gratuitous (it is not for God's private purpose) and continuous in some way with the order of the divine mind. Its life is radically grounded in God, in God's 'wisdom', to use the traditional language, and just as radically different from God (and hence vulnerable to change and chance). It is loved by God, to paraphrase St Augustine, for the sake of what God purposes to do with it; for its future, its possibility; loved *as a work*, as a product that is at once dependent and underdetermined, in process of achieving its own integrity. Hence the language of the two differences implied in Christian theology – the difference of source and outpouring in the trinitarian life, the difference of creator and creation at the level of God's relation to what is not God.[23]

So it is not a matter here of arguing incontrovertibly to God from the creative processes of our imaginations, but of noting the convergences between theological discourse and the kind of reflection on the artist's labour that these lectures have tried to trace. Human making that is more than functional, more than problem-solving, gives us some clue as to what the theologian means by creation, the setting in being of something that is both an embodiment of what is thought or conceived and also a radically independent reality with its own logic and integrity unfolding over time. And the theologian's struggling for words about the trinity gives some clue as to what might be the 'limit case' for generativity – a giving

23. There is a brilliant recent statement of this in David Bentley Hart, *The Beauty of the Infinite. The Aesthetics of Christian Truth* (Grand Rapids: Eerdmans, 2003), especially pp.155–87.

birth to what is utterly continuous ('consubstantial') and utterly other (because distinguished only by relation, not by any chance feature), both wholly drawn from the generator's substance and wholly a free re-presentation, re-realization, of the generator's life. Art helps us understand creation; the trinitarian birth of the other helps us grasp the complex relation of same to other in the artist's product.

As we reflect on this convergence and mutual illumination, one thing that comes sharply into focus is a theme that has recurred several times in these discussions. Central to 'making other' is dispossession, disinterested love. Making is necessarily a kind of withdrawal – otherwise it is repetition, the simple moving of what is 'inside' to the 'outside'. Not that this is ever a true possibility anyway; but we have seen enough argument here to make it fairly plain that it *is* possible to trivialize or corrupt the labour of making by trying to force what is made into conformity with some supposed inner concept of the work, or with a 'message', or with the self-concerned desires or anxieties of the maker. Earlier in this chapter we noted the sense in which an artist loves what is made, and the kinds of artistic effort that speak of a lack of love, a failure to allow integrity either to what is seen or to what is made. But in the context of the finite imagination – as Maritain argues, and as Hofstadter might agree – this love is always inextricably connected with self-love, since it is a form of self-discovery.[24] The artist not only uncovers what is generative in the world but also what is generative in him or herself, the alignments or attunements that make possible an art that is more than repetition or imitation. The artist discovers her own unfinishedness in the work. There is no complete self-exhaustion of the artist in what is made (remember Maritain on Rimbaud), so that there is always more that the artist can say or produce. 'Self-seeking hunter of forms' is Geoffrey Hill's apostrophe to the poetic subject; and it is true that the process of artistic production is a matter of self-discovery in some way – not in the simplistic sense of finding out what my 'real' feelings are, or some such formula, but at the more complex level where I do not know what is possible to say or do until something new has become actual. 'How do I know what I think until I see what I

24. See above, pp.24–5.

say?'[25] Art is not functional to the self, but it does *function*; and any account of what the production of art involves has to recognize that it is also the production of a self.

Art thus always approaches the condition of being both recognition and transmission of gift, gratuity or excess; but it always *approaches*. In such a perspective, we can see how the concept of divine making again acts as a limit-notion: God has nothing to discover, no self to shape. There is a sense in which God *can* be said to 'exhaust' what he is in the mutual giving of the life of the trinity.[26] Or again, the point might be pursued in relation to the doctrine of the Incarnation. The life of Christ is not a supreme case of grace given from one person to another, as it might be given

25. See Saunders Lewis, 'The poet', in Alun R. Jones and Gwyn Thomas (eds), *Presenting Saunders Lewis* (Cardiff: University of Wales Press, 1973), pp.171–6, especially p.171: 'A poem is not the expression of anything already existing.' Lewis's debt to Maritain (he was also a correspondent of David Jones) is very clear, here and elsewhere.

26. The language of self-'devastation' is used by the Russian theologian Sergii Bulgakov in his work on the Incarnation which appeared in French translation as *Du verbe incarné* (Paris: Aubier, 1943) (e.g. pp.17–20).

by God to human beings in general. Theologically, it is a bestowal of the divine identity to and through the whole existence of Jesus of Nazareth. Both the birth of the Word from the Father in eternity and the birth of Christ in time can be seen as the full 'translation' of identity into otherness without ultimate loss or alienation.

Thus when God creates the world, God acts out of a full, not an inchoate, identity. And when God deals with the world in the history of Jesus, he does not somehow seek an access of fresh experience to augment his selfhood. Thus what theology might have to say to the artist is not exactly that human creativity imitates divine but almost the opposite of this – that divine creativity is not capable of imitation; it is uniquely itself, a creation from nothing that realizes not an immanent potential in the maker but a pure desire for life and joy in what is freely made. It is the limit case of labour for the good of what is made. But though divine creation cannot be imitated, what it does is to define the nature of a love that is involved in making. It is both the *gift* of self and the gift of *self*. It bestows life unreservedly on what is other, but the life it bestows is a real selfhood, a solid reality. It is not the exercise of an arbitrary will, one subject seeking to control another.[27] God's self-identity is timeless, so that there is no sense in which God becomes more fully God in creating or in becoming human; *our* self-identity is timebound, inextricably involved with a world of interlocking causes. The most profoundly free action human beings can take in relation to their identity, the action that most fully realizes the image of God, in theological terms, is to elect to discover and mould what they are in the process of 'remaking' the world in a love that is both immeasurably different from God's (because it is to do with the self's self-definition in history and material relationship) and yet endowed with some share in it (because it is always approaching self-dispossession). Human making seeks to echo, necessarily imperfectly, the character of God's love as shown in making and becoming incarnate. In the words of a remarkable recent book on theology and aesthetics, 'Christian talk of an analogy between the being of creatures and the being of God is something like speaking of the irreducible

27. See Rowan Williams, 'On being creatures', in *On Christian Theology* (Oxford: Blackwell, 2000), pp. 63–78, for a response to criticism of the classical doctrine of creation as the imposition of an alien will.

difference between the being of a work of art and the creative being of the artist (which is not, surely, an arbitrary relationship, any more than it is "necessary").[28] The artist's freedom is deeply connected to God's; but connected as something no less deeply other to God, since it is the particular way in which finite freedom comes to perfection.

In various ways, these reflections on theologically informed art have all been to do with the connection of art and love. Maritain himself asserts that a work is 'Christian' simply to the extent that 'love is alive' in it.[29] The pivotal distinction between art and prudence that has recurred so often should not – as we have several times noted – obscure the interconnectedness of human making and the human vocation to *caritas*, to love that exhibits some participation in God's act. It would be very eccentric to see art as central to the distinctively human and at the same time as operating independently of love. The artist, as we have been reminded many times, does not need to be a saint; the point is rather that without art

28. David Bentley Hart, *op.cit.*, p.251.
29. *Art and Scholasticism*, p.71.

we should not fully see what *sanctity* is about. A holiness, a fullness of virtue, that was seen simply as a static mirroring of God's perfection would in fact not be real holiness; God's life exercises its own perfection in the imagining of a world into life, so that the exercise of the artist's imagination fills out what must be the heart of holy life for human creatures. The artist imagines a world that is both new and secretly inscribed in all that is already seen ('There is another world but it is the same as this one', in Rilke's famous phrase), and in so doing imagines himself, projects an identity that is fully in motion towards its now ungraspable completion. In this bestowing of life on self and world, the artist uncovers the generative love that is at the centre of holiness. There is no 'godlikeness' without such bestowal, such 'imagining' into life.

The artists we have been most closely examining should help us grasp the point here because, among many other things, they are conspicuously unsentimental about love. David Jones's costly turning away from one mode of representation in which he excelled in order to include more and more of the interwoven simultaneous lines of signification and allusion is an attempt to

167

embody a more radical love in what he produces, a love that attends to all the boundary-crossing echoes that characterize the real, which is also the good.[30] Flannery O'Connor strenuously denies herself a limitation to the acceptable and edifying so as to manifest the same radical love in situations that are grotesque and catastrophic. For both it is not so much that if you look after truth, beauty will look after itself as that if you work with this sort of *love*, beauty will look after itself. As Maritain insisted, beauty sought for in itself will always elude – or else it will seduce the artist into one or another sort of falsity. Given integrity of vision and purpose, consonance of component parts, and 'splendour', the active attracting summons to the viewing mind, beauty is what occurs.[31] And the combination of that integrity, consonance and radiance is the work of love, a love that has nothing at all to do with feelings of warmth and positive approbation towards what is being made but is simply the self-forgetting and urgent desire that there be real life in the product, some sort of real independence from

30. Cf. above, p.86, on David Jones's insistence on the union of the real and the good.
31. *Art and Scholasticism*, pp.23–4, 30–2, *Creative Intuition*, pp. 167–76, 183.

will and sentiment. The work 'pleases' in Maritain's sense when it has this independence; it is beautiful when it is released from the artist.

We have come some way from the details of criticism, visual or poetic, and some way even from Maritain's formal and philosophical sketch of the artist's labour. But none of those we have been discussing would have been surprised or dismayed to find that we had ended up with some directly doctrinal concerns and themes. All believed that art was as it was because reality was as it was; and the way reality is would be unintelligible without the doctrine of God that Christian theologians have elaborated, a doctrine that puts gift and dispossession at the foundation of everything. If art is indeed an acute case of knowledge in general, as suggested earlier in this chapter, if it is a manifestation of the deeper levels of participatory knowledge, it must, for any religious believer, be bound up with the being and action of God. As I have said, I don't intend to argue that only Christian theology can make sense of art; but the tradition I have been examining would claim that theology has, as we might put it, a story to tell about artistic labour which provides a ground for certain features of it and challenges it to be faithful to certain canons of disinterest and integrity. That this helps to foster art which is intensely serious, unconsoling, and unafraid of the complexity of a world that the secularist too can recognize might persuade us to give a little more intellectual house-room to the underlying theology than we might at first be inclined to offer. David Jones and Flannery O'Connor have a good case to be regarded as artists who do not use religious vision as a short cut of any kind; there are others, of whom Dostoevsky, a significant presence in the margins of much that has been written here, is only one. If, as I suggested at the beginning of this study, we need some serious thinking about what counts as artistic labour, in relation to what counts as *human* labour, we could find many worse and less probing interlocutors.

Index of Names